MENTORING STUDENTS AT RISK

ABOUT THE AUTHOR

Gary Reglin is an associate research scholar/scientist. He is director of the Escambia School District Mentoring and Tutoring Help (M.A.T.H.) program, the Santa Rosa School District Mentor Program, and the coordinator of the Alternative Educator Training program in the College of Education (Educational Research and Development Center) at the University of West Florida in Pensacola, Florida.

Dr. Reglin managed a successful dropout-retention program in Florida public schools. This program was featured on television and in the February 1990 edition of *Technological Horizons in Education Journal* (T.H.E.). Dr. Reglin's 40 publications are in such refereed journals as the *National Association of Secondary School Principals (NASSP) Bulletin, High School Journal, Middle School League Journal, Journal of At-Risk Issues,* and *The School Administrator.* He presented at 26 refereed national and state conferences. He has published three books: *Motivating Low-Achieving Students: A Special Focus on Unmotivated and Underachieving African-American Students; At-Risk "Parent and Family" Involvement: Strategies for Low-Income Families and African-American Families of Unmotivated and Underachieving Students;* and *Achievement for African-American Students: Strategies for the Diverse Classroom.* The author is the associate editor of the *Journal of At-Risk Issues* and serves on the editorial boards of several journals, including the *Journal of Research on Minority Affairs.* In the Eastern Educational Research Association, he chairs the special interest group on *Policies for the Management and Training of Teachers* and serves on the board of directors. The author teaches graduate courses such as *Advanced Issues in Working with Students At Risk.*

MENTORING STUDENTS AT RISK

An Underutilized Alternative Education Strategy for K-12 Teachers

By

GARY REGLIN, ED.D.
Associate Research Scholar
College of Education
Educational Research and Development Center
University of West Florida
Pensacola, Florida

CHARLES C THOMAS • PUBLISHER, LTD.
Springfield • Illinois • USA

Published and Distributed Throughout the World by
CHARLES C THOMAS • PUBLISHER, LTD.
2600 South First Street
Springfield, Illinois 62794-9265

© *1998 by* CHARLES C THOMAS • PUBLISHER, LTD.
ISBN 0-398-06833-X

Library of Congress Catalog Card Number: 97-37061

*With THOMAS BOOKS careful attention is given to all details of manufacturing
and design. It is the Publisher's desire to present books that are satisfactory as to their
physical qualities and artistic possibilities and appropriate for their particular use.
THOMAS BOOKS will be true to those laws of quality that assure a good name and
good will.*

Printed in the United States of America
MS-R-3

Library of Congress Cataloging in Publication Data

Reglin, Gary.
    Mentoring students at risk: an underutilized alternative education
strategy for K-12 teachers / by Gary Reglin.
            p.   cm.
    Includes bibliographical references (p.)
    ISBN 0-398-06833-X (paper)
    1. Socially handicapped children–Education–United States.
2. Socially handicapped youth–Education–United States.
3. Mentoring in education–United States.   4. Dropouts–United
States–Prevention.   I. Title.
LC4091.R417   1998
371.93'086'94–dc21

With love and thankfulness, I dedicate this book to my family, and in particular to my son, Sebastian, my daughter, Kedra, and in memory of my father, Willie James.

PREFACE

This publication is the result of my numerous requests from teachers to collaborate with them to establish mentoring programs for students at risk in their schools. Teachers begin to realize what research has demonstrated for many years. Research clearly shows mentoring is a powerful alternative education (dropout prevention) strategy for students at risk.

Chapter One discusses the need to restructure classrooms, programs, and schools to better serve our students. Why restructure? The answer is twofold. First, there exists more research-based, effective alternative education programs to use as models. Second, some school boards of education are mostly ignoring the at-risk situation by not being proactive in pursuing alternative education. It is imperative that teachers take a leadership role to bring alternative education into their schools. Teachers have to be proactive on the issue of alternative education.

Common questions asked by teachers are: Who are these students at risk? Why mark these students with the at-risk label? Answers to these questions are shared in Chapter One. The chapter also delineates important facts about alternative education, specifically that alternative education is research-based; alternative education schools are personal and focused; and alternative education students feel valued. Lastly, the chapter explains five commonly used categories of alternative education programs: Educational Alternative Programs, Teenage Parent Programs, Substance Abuse Programs, Disciplinary Programs, and Youth Services Programs.

Chapter Two introduces two funded alternative education programs with which the author works. The programs are the Truancy Court Conference Program (T.C.C.P.) and the Mentoring and Tutoring Help

(M.A.T.H.) Program.

With the inception of the Truancy Court Conference Program (T.C.C.P.) came the first system to document, monitor, and process truants. The Mentoring and Tutoring Help (M.A.T.H.) program provides positive role models from the community for the Truancy Court Conference Program students. Involving these students in a personal relationship with the mentor and in school activities with the mentor engenders renewed interest in school and a feeling of belonging. The mentoring component of the M.A.T.H. program produces substantial successes in proteges.

A significant portion of the M.A.T.H. program can be used by K-12 teachers to establish mentoring programs in their school districts. For instance, teachers can use the M.A.T.H. organizational chart and the TimeTable of Major M.A.T.H. Milestones as models to design similar instruments for their mentoring programs.

Chapter Three discusses some more important components of the M.A.T.H. program. These components are helpful to teachers to design, operate, and evaluate their mentoring programs. *Tips* to help recruit, screen, and orient mentors are presented. Models to design recruiting flyers, mentor applications, and interest inventories are shared, as well as mentor interview questions.

Activities for mentors and proteges are delineated to include community service activities. The latter part of this chapter shares process and outcome evaluation questions. The procedure for the M.A.T.H process and outcome evaluation is helpful to teachers. Lastly, a 20-Step Replicable Model for Students At Risk will be supportive of teachers' efforts to design and to write a proposal to fund their program. The model summarizes the important features of the M.A.T.H. program, which are applicable to most school-based mentoring programs.

Chapter Four deals with what K-12 teachers can emphasize to mentors. In this chapter, the need for teachers to facilitate the efforts of mentors to gain knowledge and training in specific areas is discussed. The areas are familiarity with theories on school achievement, sincerity about helping, committing for the long-term, bonding, reliability, praising and listening, dos and don'ts, terminating if needed, liabilities, communicating with teachers, and setting goals and objectives.

Chapter Five deals with *tips* for teachers to build a mentoring program. These *tips* are organized into distinct categories. The categories are familiarity with effective mentoring programs; identifying proteges and school liaison persons; writing mission statements, goals, and objectives; and being aware of the changed family structure and a facilitator of family involvement.

ACKNOWLEDGMENTS

This book, like almost all others, could not have been written without invaluable support from many people. The author wishes to express his gratitude and thanks to all those who gave assistance as he gathered this information. Special acknowledgment goes to Cheryl Mallory and Terry Bell. Cheryl works with programs for students at risk at Pensacola Junior College in Pensacola, Florida. Terry works in the Educational Research and Development Center at the University of West Florida. Cheryl and Terry critiqued the manuscript and contributed many ideas which enhanced all of the chapters.

Special thanks go to Stacy Jobling, coordinator of the Escambia School District Mentoring and Tutoring Help (M.A.T.H.) program, and Anjanette "Anjie" Moffitt, coordinator of the Santa Rosa School District Mentor Program. Stacy and Anjie field-tested the data collection instruments in the text. They innovated and critiqued many of the recruitment, screening, orientation, and training procedures in Chapters Two and Three.

I would like to acknowledge Deborah Malishan and Elainia "Helen" Adams for their contributions. Deborah is the principal of Lincoln Park Elementary School in Escambia County, Florida. Elainia is the principal of Pleasant Grove Elementary School in Escambia County, Florida. Both are adjunct professors at the University of West Florida, and they teach courses in our Master's Degree program in Alternative Education. Deborah and Elainia completed a thorough review of strategies and models in Chapter Four, carefully pointing out what would work and would not work for K-12 teachers. Lastly, this book was supported in part by grants and contracts from the American Express and Travel Related Services, the International Paper Foundation, the Escambia Public School District, and the Santa Rosa Public School District.

CONTENTS

MENTORING STUDENTS AT RISK

CHAPTER 1

TEACHERS CAN RESTRUCTURE EDUCATION FOR STUDENTS AT RISK

OBJECTIVES

After reading this chapter, teachers should be able to:

- Explain why restructuring education is important for students at risk.
- List the research-based alternative education strategies used with students at risk.
- Explain why increasing time on task results in more achievement for students at risk.
- Discuss the outcome of students at risk being ignored.
- Tell what the term *at-risk* means.
- Explain why truancy often leads to juvenile delinquency.
- Discuss why juvenile crimes and gangs are on the increase.
- Provide statistics to show that dropouts are costly to society.
- Define or describe the term *alternative education.*
- Discuss some important research studies supporting alternative education.
- Explain how alternative education schools are more flexible than regular schools.
- Compare and contrast the five categories of alternative education programs.

WHY RESTRUCTURE?

Nationally, many schools are going to the school-based management approach to school governance. School-based management formally alters school governance arrangements. Decision-making authority is redistributed for the purpose of stimulating and sustaining school improvements in individual schools, resulting in an increase in authority of teachers at the school (Duttweiler, 1995).

School-based management gives teachers at school sites the authority to make important decisions about personnel, staff development, allocation of resources, curriculum, and instruction. Thus, teachers can become major players in efforts to restructure classroom instruction and school programs to better serve students at risk. Students at risk are defined as those students who are seen as potentially dropping out of school for various reasons. Reasons vary, including low self-esteem, drug abuse, problems within the family unit, pregnancy, behavioral problems, interaction skills, and the like.

As teachers know so well, there is a dire need to restructure education for students at risk. Presently, the system is failing students. According to the National Assessment of Educational Progress (1985), almost a quarter of all seventeen-year-old students cannot read simple magazines. Since approximately 14 percent of students drop out by age seventeen, the problem becomes enormous (Slavin, 1989).

Orr (1987) revealed that subpar academic performance includes many personal and social pressures that have long been known to negatively affect educational achievement and school completion. More specifically, Peng (1983) identified family-related problems such as getting divorced or married, being pregnant, needing to work, as well as personal problems such as being sick, responding to peer pressure, becoming violent, and lacking self-esteem as reasons for poor achievement and premature school departure.

Teachers know that the argument for restructuring rests, for the most part, on the fact that America's schools have reached a point where minor changes or improvements to the current system will be inadequate. Changes must be fundamental and cost effective. In making their case, some point to the fairly dismal record of American schoolchildren in the past 25 years (Wircenski, Sarkees, & West 1990); others refer to the outdated *factory model* of schooling in which students are processed, as on an assembly line (Fiske, 1991). Still others cite the increasing diversity of students and the way they learn (Reglin, 1995) or the heavily bureaucratized system of public education (Finn, 1991).

My research and personal experiences show teachers becoming more aggressive in restructuring classrooms and schools to reflect more alternative education. All teachers must restructure for two basic reasons. First, there are more validated alternative education strategies. Second, many school boards of education are neither knowledgeable nor proactive when it comes to alternative education. In fact, for various reasons, some school boards of education largely ignore the at-risk situation.

More Validated Alternative Education Strategies

According to Morley (1993), alternative education is a perspective. It is based upon the belief that there are many ways to become educated, as well as many types of environments and structures within which this may occur. Alternative education means recognizing that everyone does not learn in the same way and, therefore, that some should be taught differently using an innovative curriculum. This is especially true for students at risk. It means accepting that all classrooms, programs, and schools do not have to be alike with the same learning environments. Therefore, it is a means of instituting variety and choice within school systems. Today, some public school districts have done well in implementing alternative education. Many of the alternative education efforts were designed with significant input from classroom teachers.

Thirty years ago, the curriculum field had almost nothing to offer the student at risk in terms of school restructuring. Today, we have an array of validated strategies that we can pass on to novice and experienced teachers, to school policy-makers, and to legislators. Scores of such alternative education strategies have been revealed by the research, which can substantially increase the effectiveness and productivity of schools and reduce educational costs. Below is a list of important research-based alternative education strategies.

List of Research-Based Alternative Education Strategies

- Modified scheduling
- Common planning periods for teachers
- Peer tutoring and peer teaching
- Individualized instruction
- Career awareness
- Self-concept and affective education
- Manipulatives
- Service learning projects
- Authentic assessments
- Summer enrichment program
- Teachers-As-Advisors
- Learning styles instruction
- Teacher aides
- Anger management curriculum
- Conflict resolution curriculum
- Whole-child instruction
- Self-esteem building
- Resource speakers
- Challenging goals and feedback
- Team/core teaching
- Peer counseling
- Peer mediation
- Award systems
- Vocational assessment/experiences
- Application of life skills
- Field trips
- Computer Assisted Instruction
- Internet
- Adopt-A-Student
- Multiple Intelligences
- Low student/teacher ratio
- Student portfolios
- Violence prevention curriculum
- Social skills curriculum
- Competency based instruction
- Enhanced Time on Task Techniques
- Establishing Challenging goals
- Mentoring

The latter three alternative education strategies (Enhanced Time on Task Techniques, Establishing Challenging Goals, and Mentoring) will be discussed briefly. Information on many of these strategies can be obtained by reading two of my books: *Achievement for African-American Students* and *Motivating Low-Achieving Students*. Information on the publishers of both books is in the Index of this book.

Increasing Time on Task

The actual amount of time during which students are actively engaged in learning varies enormously from one classroom to another and from one student to another. Most studies indicate that the average student is *on task* for about one-third to one-half of his/her time in school. My research and personal experiences show that these numbers are much greater for students at risk. Some students at risk learn slowly only because they are off task much of the time.

There are techniques teachers can use to increase students' at risk time on task. One technique is to minimize interruptions and disruptions in instruction. Another is to plan routines that provide for quick transitions during and at the beginning and end of classes. Other strategies include making the instructional material interesting and meaningful, providing frequent feedback, facilitating successes, incorporating frequent low-key assessment, minimizing individual seatwork, and using active methods of instruction. Still, other strategies include using mentors to increase attendance and tutors to help with students' classroom work. With these strategies, it is a relatively simple matter for teachers to increase average time on task for students at risk, hence, increasing educational effectiveness by 30 or 40 percent.

Establishing Challenging Goals

As a result of their undergraduate and graduate studies, usually teachers are familiar with a new psychological theory that has been developed over the past thirty years. This theory, the Goal Theory, is one of the most valid theories, if not the most valid theory, of work motivation. However, the Goal Theory is still largely ignored by educators. My research and personal experiences show that the Goal Theory is very relevant to the learning of students at risk.

The Goal Theory has identified a type of motivation distinct from either intrinsic or extrinsic motivation: goal motivation. If a student at risk is assigned, and accepts, an understandable, feasible goal, that goal will be itself a primary incentive to performance.

Goal Theory research has shown that difficult goals produce superior performance to easy goals, and that goals with feedback are more effective than either goals or feedback alone. Effect sizes in this research are in the order of .50 to .80, which makes this a highly productive alternative education strategy. In educational practice, this means teachers establishing clear, meaningful and challenging goals, and giving immediate and frequent feedback.

Mentoring in K-12 Schools

The term mentor encompasses a variety of roles: advocate, buddy and friend (Kwalick, 1988). Mentoring is defined as a sustained relationship between a caring adult and a student. The research literature on mentoring is unique in that it is unanimously positive. The empirical results show a fairly modest but consistent effect size on academic achievement of about .40 (Flaxman, 1992). The effect is greater if the mentors are somewhat older (three years or more) than the protégés. Mentoring, including tutoring, has consistent effects on the academic attainment of all students. It is a particularly encouraging experience for students who may be underachieving academically.

Nationally, teachers are collaborating with universities, government agencies, businesses, and the military to plan, fund, implement, and evaluate mentoring programs in their classrooms and in their schools. On many occasions, I coordinated grant proposal planning meetings with teams of teachers who contributed significantly to every phase of planning the mentoring program.

Teachers decide the number of mentors needed, the number of mentoring hours per week, the students and classes requiring mentors, parking spaces for mentors, school contact persons, data collection procedures, funding agencies to target, and the like. Teachers' input resulted in a high degree of success with potential funders.

In large part, due to this collaboration between my university and the teachers, funding was received for mentoring programs from diverse sources to include: private foundations, federal agencies, state agencies, and local school boards. The funding facilitates the operation of a research-based mentoring program with a budget to hire a coordinator, train mentors, conduct background screening, pay mentors a stipend, and conduct a good program evaluation.

School Boards Ignore At-Risk Situation

Despite the efforts of advocates of alternative education, such as me, there are a substantial number of public school districts which have no comprehensive alternative education plan for dealing with the at-risk situation. For the most part, these school districts are ignoring the at-risk situation. Hence, the gap has widened between students at risk and their higher-achieving peers (Lehr & Harris, 1994).

Demographic data show growth in the population of students facing school failure, expulsion, or high dropout potential. Complicated economic and social forces exacerbate problems experienced by these students. This results in increased special learning needs and calls for more structured remediation through alternative education programs.

A learned colleague of mine informed me that, in part, the at-risk situation is being ignored because many school educators do not understand the term, *students at risk.* My research and personal experiences confirm this assumption.

During the late 1980s, educators began to use the term at-risk to describe certain categories of students. The 1989 Phi Delta Kappa study of students at risk began with the assumption that students are at risk if they are likely to fail either in school or in life (Frymeir & Gansneder, 1989). Lehr and Harris (1994) explained that a review of the literature does not show a formally accepted definition of the student at risk, but they later define the student at risk as a student who is not working up to potential. The term *at-risk* seems to encompass many groups of students who have characteristics or needs that require additional learning alternatives due to retention in grade, expulsion from school, dropping out of school, or other factors.

Miller (1993) reports that the term *at-risk* has entered the educational vernacular with a vengeance. Every time it is invoked it refers to a different subcategory of student. Having multiple definitions for *at-risk* make maintaining focus and understanding problematic.

Ogden and Ferminario (1988) believe all children are occasionally students at-risk. However, there is a segment of every school population that consistently shows a lack of the intellectual, emotional, and social skills necessary to take full advantage of the educational opportunities available to them. This dysfunctional segment of the student population typically has educational deficiencies and needs due to poor basic skills attainment, learning problems, low grades, disciplinary problems, and high absenteeism. These students may have been referred to a student support team or assigned to an alternative education program as a result of their deficiencies.

WHO ARE STUDENTS AT RISK?

Common questions I hear from K-12 teachers are: Who are these students at risk? Why mark these students with the at-risk label? A meta-analysis of extant research by Frymier (1989) identified forty-five factors that contribute to students being at-risk. Of these, only retention is the direct result of low achievement in school. Retention, in turn, increases the probability of dropping out of school. Holmes and Matthews (1984) found that retention practices continue despite research showing that the potential for negative effects consistently outweighs positive outcomes. Their study concluded that proponents of retention plans should have to show the pedagogical logic behind their policies in light of the discouraging empirical evidence.

One purpose served by the at-risk label is identification of categories of persons who are at-risk. Thus, the study of children at risk may enable us to identify and intervene in student behavior that leads to failure in school before retention, expulsion or school dropout occurs (Richardson, Casanova, Placier, & Guilfoyle, 1989). The concern for children at risk today reflects our nation's reawakening to the causes and consequences of grade retention, school expulsion, and dropout within society (Pellicano, 1987).

Pellicano concludes that it has become fashionable to identify children at risk in terms of poverty, alcohol and drug consumption, sexual activity, school attendance, educational failure, race, and ethnicity. Causes of the condition include the breakdown of the family, the unwillingness or inability of the government and schools to meet their responsibilities to children, the permissiveness of society's value system, or the absence of values in the home or school.

Slavin (1989) defines students at risk as students who, on the basis of identified characteristics or needs, are unlikely to graduate or leave school with the basic skills because of school failure. My review of literature reveals that Slavin has the most comprehensive definition of students at risk. Therefore, I encourage all K-12 teachers to use Slavin's definition to facilitate defining students at risk in their alternative education efforts. Usually, alternative education programs serve many different categories of students at risk including: juvenile delinquents, truants, gang members, dropouts, and pregnant teens.

Juvenile Delinquents

Juvenile delinquency has become a high priority in many states throughout the nation. The national, state, and local funding available for research-based alternative education programs to serve juvenile delinquents is significant.

U.S. courts with juvenile jurisdiction handled 1,471,200 cases of delinquency in 1992 with a disproportionate increase in violent offenses (e.g., 80% more aggravated assaults, 86% more charges involving weapons). This figure represents a 26 percent increase in delinquency cases since 1988.

Studies of juveniles who committed crimes indicate that these offenders share several common characteristics: (1) are four to five years behind in education and social skills, (2) have single parent and/or disadvantaged families, (3) are substance abusers, and (4) have siblings who have been or are involved in crime. One study of 2,670 juvenile offenders shows that the average student, while 15 years, six months of age at the time of testing and in the ninth grade, was reading at a fourth grade level. Thirty-eight percent of all students scored below fourth grade.

Considering the aforementioned facts, it is not surprising that an estimated 90,000 status offenses (truancy, ungovernable, runaway, liquor) were formally disposed of by U.S. courts with juvenile jurisdiction in 1991. This represents a 9 percent increase from 1987. The largest increase among the four major status offenses was for petitioned truancy cases, an increase of 22 percent between 1987 and 1991. Oftentimes, teachers find themselves working in or collaborating with alternative education programs which serve delinquents.

Truant Students Become Juvenile Delinquents

Research shows that truancy is associated with juvenile delinquency and deviant behaviors, to include drug and alcohol abuse, criminal behavior, marital problems, and violence. Truancy greatly increases the probability of becoming a high school dropout. Each year's class of dropouts will cost the nation an estimated $240 billion in lost earnings and foregone taxes over their lifetimes, which does not include the estimated billions for crime control, welfare, health care, and other social services.

Much of public debate about delinquency centers on targeting truant youth. The old adage *an ounce of prevention is worth a pound of cure* seems especially applicable to these youth. Over the past several years, legislators have begun to recognize the need for prevention. In 1992, the Juvenile and Delinquency Prevention Act of 1974 was amended to expand the role of the Office of Juvenile Justice and Delinquency Programs. The expanded role is a federal effort to prevent and treat juvenile delinquency and improve the juvenile justice system by focusing on three priorities: improved state and local communities to prevent youth from entering the justice system, improved state and local administration of justice and services to juveniles, and strengthened families of delinquents. The amendment encourages coordination of services, interagency cooperation, truancy prevention programs, and parental involvement in treatment and services for juveniles.

Hooky Playing Students *Ain't* Cool in the '90s

Playing hooky from school is a phenomenon that has been treated as comical behavior in many segments of American popular culture. Tom Sawyer and Huck Finn did it and folks thought it was cool. When the Little Rascals did it, the resultant chase scenes with Spanky, Alfalfa, and Buckwheat running from the truant officer made moviegoers laugh. Unfortunately, truancy is not as comical as art has made it out to be (Stopp, 1996). In public schools, truancy is highly correlated with low levels of school achievement and with high dropout rates.

Truant and Delinquent Students

The case for providing a better education for truant and delinquent students rests on three basic arguments. First, the national economy will increasingly depend upon an educated work force for its health (Richman, 1991). Moreover, demographic projections show minority workers and women occupying an ever larger portion of the work force (Hodgkinson, 1991). A disproportionate number of truant and delinquent students are African-American, Hispanic-American, and Native-American students. Second, American competitiveness in a global marketplace depends upon the ability of our high school and college graduates to efficiently design and produce high-quality goods. Third, the deterioration of American cities and increases in crime, substance abuse, and poverty can, in part, be attributed to a decline in the educational level and economic status of the nation's youth.

Truant and delinquent children are no longer confined to a few urban ghetto schools or a few rural trailer parks, but are now part of mainstream America. Indeed, the factors which make children truant and delinquent have spread to every community: poverty, weak family structure, subpar parent education, substance abuse, and crime (National Center for Education Statistics, 1990).

Juvenile Delinquents in Florida

It is important for K-12 teachers to become familiar with the statistics associated with juvenile delinquency and juvenile crime in their respective states. I have analyzed these statistics for Florida. Florida's statistics give K-12 teachers a view of how grim the delinquency and crime problem is.

Florida ranks 49th in the nation for juvenile crime, having 751 violent criminal arrests per thousand in 1992 while the national average was 483 per thousand. By comparison, in Florida, the 1985 rate was 480 per thousand versus the national rate of 305. These statistics reveal that Florida suffered a juvenile crime rate in 1985 that many other states did not encounter until 1992. Florida's dropout rate was 11.9 percent compared to the national rate of 9.3 percent. It is, therefore, no surprise that Florida has received nationwide media attention about its youth, both in areas of education and crime.

Gangs

The formation of gangs has been part of human existence throughout the centuries. One can easily recall legends and fables about gangs such as pirates, Robin Hood and his men, the Jesse James gang, and Al Capone, who banded with others primarily for financial profit. More contemporary stories of gangs are West Side Story, Colors, and Straight Out of Brooklyn. A gang image can vary from one of violence and illegal activity to one as simple as a play group like Spanky and Our Gang. In our society the term gang indicates, at minimum, mischievousness.

Goldstein and Huff (1993) define a gang as closely or loosely organized association of individuals who express their identification through private language, symbolic behavior, and the wearing of *colors* and who commonly claim territory in a neighborhood. The gang and its individual members tend to engage in criminal behavior primarily, though not exclusively, as a function of the association.

The impact of youth gangs on school can be concluded from many reports of violence in and near schools. A 1988 survey of superintendents and representatives of 17 of the country's major school districts identified three major safety problems: drugs, gangs, and weapons. Also observed is that the severity of violence has increased, particularly with the impact of drugs and gangs. School incidents are considered to be gang related when they are directed by gang leadership or consensus by the members; the behavior benefits the gang; gang motivation is present (displaying of colors, shouting gang phrases, displaying gang's symbols during the act); or the incident is in response to another gang's activity or threat (Goldstein & Huff, 1993).

Crime and gangs are on the increase in nearly every county throughout the United States. For instance, in my county (Escambia County), in northwest Florida, there were few reported gangs several years ago. Now, the newspaper consistently publishes articles on gang activity in Escambia County.

Escambia County is 75 percent white, 20 percent black, 2 percent Asian, 2 percent Hispanic, and 1 percent other. It is a high crime area with a low percentage of high school graduates. About 43,400 students attend the county's 70 public schools. There are forty-five elementary schools, ten middle schools, eight high schools, and seven special centers.

Why the increase in gangs in Escambia County? The increase in gangs is highly correlated with the increase in juvenile crime. According to the district *Crime and Violence Report for School Year 1994-1995*, a record number of students had encounters with the law. There were 4,077 such encounters: homicide, robbery, arson, malicious harassment/hate crimes, sexual battery, motor theft, and assault. A report from the Court Liaison Officer for Escambia County Schools shows 3,618 juvenile arrests were made from June 1995 to May 1996: 81 arrests in the elementary schools, 724 arrests in the middle schools, 1,770 arrests in the high schools, and 1,043 arrests in the alternative programs.

The incidence of juvenile crime in Escambia County made it one of ten counties in the state selected by the Florida Department of Law Enforcement to participate in a Serious Habitual Offender Comprehensive Action Program for juveniles, a distinction normally afforded to only the largest, most populated counties in Florida, i.e., Dade, Broward, Palm Beach, Hillsborough, etc. Escambia county's juvenile crime rates are displayed in Table I.

Table I: Escambia County Juvenile Crime Rate

Escambia County Juvenile Crime Rate		
Year	**Number of Cases**	**% Increase**
1990-1991	2,639	-
1991-1992	2,849	20%
1992-1993	2,997	5%
1993-1994	3,149	5%
1994-1995	3,735	19%
Felonies		
From:	**To:**	**% Increase**
1993-1994	1994-1995	16%
Felony Drug Offences		
From:	**To:**	**% Increase**
1993-1994	1994-1995	41%
Misdemeanors		
From:	**To:**	**% Increase**
1993-1994	1994-1995	12%

A Grand Jury investigation in the county, beginning June 20, 1995, reported that there are at least four or five hundred young people who are members of various gangs. There are 24 different gangs. The Grand Jury determined that national gangs are being established in the county at a rapid pace. It recommended a task force be established to address the local gang problem.

Why do students join gangs? The most commonly cited reasons by gang members for joining a gang include protection, status, identity, access to friends, a feeling of family, protection of the neighborhood, and access to girls (Goldstein & Huff, 1993). Hopelessness, negative role models, and poor self-esteem are contributing factors for gang involvement (Conly, 1993).

Gang membership fulfills the need youth have to belong to something. They may need to identify with and have the approval of other men/boys because there is usually no father figure in the home. These boys are looking for a male model to emulate (Congressional

Oversight Hearing of Local Gang Diversion Programs. 1993).

Youth associated with gangs need a cadre of people who can relate to them, help them solve problems, be supportive in times of stress, and intervene with and for them when crises occur. A strong mentor support network provides alternatives to ineffective family units or negative influences that lead youth to antisocial and criminal behaviors (Goldstein, 1991).

Clay Hollopeter, Executive of the Boy's Club of El Monte, California, developed three approaches to helping gang youth that have been substantially successful (Congressional Oversight Hearing on Local Gang Diversion Programs, 1993). These three approaches are (1) an individualized program of service; (2) a network of supportive service providers, agencies, and referrals; and (3) advocacy on behalf of the youth.

Mentoring programs are excellent interventions to satisfy the needs of youth who have potential or actual gang involvement. Mentoring programs help society to effectively grapple with the overwhelming problem of gangs and gang mentality. These programs allow us to think in more human and immediate terms. Congressman Matthew Martinez revealed, during the Congressional Oversight Hearings on Local Gang Diversion Programs, that mentoring programs offer summer employment to college students who can become both tutors and role models to the project's enrollees. These enrollees would receive valuable one-on-one help to strengthen their academic weaknesses.

In summary, mentoring meets the needs of potential or actual gang members. An effective mentoring relationship satisfies the need for protection with advocacy, identity with positive role models and eventual autonomy, a feeling of belonging through social bonding, and a need for status (success) with academic accomplishments.

Dropouts Are a Crisis

A dropout is defined as a person who has left the educational institution, has not graduated, and is not currently enrolled in regular school anywhere. Every child in the United States today is entitled to an education. Each year, however, thousands of young people drop out of school. These students are the *forgotten half*, the *at-risk*, that the school system seems to have overlooked. These students who dropout are from all walks of life, all parts of the county, and of all nationalities. Their lack of appropriate education targets them as unproductive and a drain on the country's resources.

Dropping out of school is costly (Reglin, 1990). Students who drop out lost at least one-third of their potential income. Dropping out of school increases the chances of incarceration three to nine times. The cost of incarceration for dropouts was at least three times that of educating students for a given year (Reglin, 1993a).

In many states, the dropout situation is shocking. For instance, the dropout rate in Florida is at a crisis point. The dropout rate in Florida was 12 percent, compared to a national rate of 9 percent (Florida Kids Count Data Book, 1994). Many school districts struggle with the dropout crisis. For instance, in my county, Escambia County, the number of nonpromotions (failed students) was 1,064. There were 9,092 disciplinary actions, 3,000 in-school suspensions, and 5,066 out of school suspensions. The graduation rate in Escambia County in 1994 was only 68.5 percent.

The Florida Statistical Abstract, page 128, Table 4.28, reflects the number of secondary public school students on free and reduced lunch. About 60 percent of all students in Escambia County are on free or reduced lunch; 25,104 students on free lunch and 4,181 on reduced lunches. Poverty and teenage pregnancy contribute significantly to the high dropout rate in most counties, similar to as in my county.

Poverty and Teenage Pregnancy Contribute to Dropouts

With a population of 263,000, Escambia County is one of the nation's poorest areas. The poverty rate is 29.9 percent for children under age six and 26.2 percent for children under age 18 (Florida Kids Count Data Book, 1994). Thirty-nine percent of the population is eligible for Medicaid and 34 percent of the population is on food stamps. Furthermore, statistics show that $21,518,923 was spent in Escambia on Aid to Families with Dependent Children (AFDC) in Fiscal year 1992-1993. Over 14 percent of the population receives AFDC payments.

Children are the victims. The 1995 Florida Statistical Abstract, page 100, depicts the number of births to teenagers in 67 counties in Florida. Only 10 counties had more births to teenagers than Escambia County.

Our teenage pregnancy rate is at the crisis stage. The teen birth rate per 1,000 (ages 15-19) in Florida is 64.4 percent; this rate is 70.9 percent in Escambia County (Florida Kids Count Data Book, 1994). Children born out of wedlock in Florida is 34.2 percent. Escambia County's is 37.2 percent.

Approximately half of Escambia County's teen mothers drop out of school and start a cycle of poverty which makes them dependent upon society. It is a serious economic, social, and health crisis in the county and in the state of Florida. Teen childbearing in Florida in 1991 cost Florida taxpayers $92.1 million.

ALTERNATIVE EDUCATION: TEACHERS' RESTRUCTURING SOLUTION

What is a solution for the aforementioned problems plaguing our children in Escambia County, in Florida, and in the nation? What is a solution for a public school system which is failing many of our students? The answer is alternative education. Alternative education is a set of strategies, beliefs, and support services that facilitate growth in academic, personal/social, and career development initiatives (Chalker, 1996). Alternative education is defined as another form of education with variations of services and offerings available to specific groups of students whose needs are not being met in traditional classes.

Raywid (1994) noted that two enduring consistencies characterized alternative schools from the start: they have been designed to respond to a group that appears not to be optimally serviced by the regular program, and consequently they have represented varying degrees of departure from standard school organization, programs, and environments. Bucci and Reitzammer (1992) found that positive attitudes on the part of all teachers, parents, students, and community members contribute a supportive school climate essential for effective alternative education.

Traditional education is appropriate for a majority of students, but for those who do not respond to the contemporary forms of education, alternatives should be offered. Public educators have to try to meet the needs of all children in our schools. Alternative education programs may offer the best hope for meeting the needs of students at risk.

Bucci and Rietzammer (1992) found alternative programs to be worthwhile for students at risk at the secondary level. Since the traditional classroom is not always the best learning environment for students at risk, they often benefit from alternative education, which provides opportunities to learn in other settings. It is vital that alternative education classes, programs, and schools be small, located in a non-traditional setting, foster a close working relationship between staff and students, emphasize support and encouragement, employ a comprehensive and multifaceted service approach, emphasize improvement of basic skills and self-esteem, and include work experience or other types of experiential learning.

Hefner-Packer (1991) describes alternative education as an educational strategy, classroom, program, or school designed to provide learning experiences that meet student needs in a positive environment using strategies that may be more structured or less structured than traditional educational programs. Beck (1991) believes that alternative education programs help schools meet the needs of students who have delinquent behavior, who have withdrawn from school, who lack fundamental basic skills, and/or those for whom the regular curriculum is boring or inappropriate. Beck identifies special courses or programs, schools-within-a-school, or separate schools as viable alternatives. Individualized instruction is a key to the success of alternative education.

Alternative education is an excellent restructuring solution for several reasons: it is widely supported by respected organizations such as the National Dropout Prevention Network; it is research based; alternative educations schools are personable and focused; and alternative education students feel valued.

National Dropout Prevention Network Support Alternative Education

In a recent survey of 454 members of the National Dropout Prevention Network by the National Dropout Prevention Center at Clemson University, 74.5 percent of the respondents listed alternative school environments as being highly to moderately effective for high-risk students (Duttweiler, 1994). When properly established and properly implemented, alternative schools and alternative strategies were effective dropout prevention interventions (Morley, 1993). These schools and strategies recognize that everyone did not learn in the same way and that everyone should not be taught in the same way using a common curriculum.

Alternative Education Is Research Based

Research demonstrates that there are certain characteristics present in alternative education which are successful with students who do not prosper in the regular education. It is clear that successful alternative classes, programs, and school have the following characteristics: (a) they are small and have low teacher/pupil ratios; (b) they have faculties that develop caring relationships with students; (c) they set forth clear rules; (d) they have high expectations for student achievement; (e) they foster positive peer relationships; and (f) they develop students' self-esteem. Students who might otherwise drop out of school and become problems to society become productive adults with the help of understanding and caring alternative education teachers.

My review of literature reveals that every year a substantial number of K-12 teachers use the same traditional instructional practices in the regular school settings. I observed these traditional practices of teaching and learning at a newly established rural Alternative Center for Education in rural North Carolina in February 1994. I was concerned because these traditional practices reinforced *at-risk-ness* (Manning, 1993).

Constant use of the traditional practices has to cease. There is a substantial amount of research and practice validating the effectiveness of alternative education instructional practices (Florida Department of Education, 1996). Students at risk academic success factors (grades, attendance, behavior, etc.) improve more in an alternative education setting as compared with a regular education setting.

Until the late 1980s, the research base for alternative education was dependent on studies conducted during the 1970s. In a review of this early research, Young (1990) discussed a study by Gold and Mann on the academic achievement and attitudes of delinquent students. The researchers compared approximately 60 at-risk students from three alternative secondary schools with a matched group of students from conventional secondary schools in the same districts. The study found the following:

- Alternative education students were significantly less disruptive in school at the end of the study than conventional students.
- Teachers rated alternative education students who returned to conventional schools as slightly better behaved than conventional students.
- Alternative education students were significantly more positive about school and confident in their role as students than conventional students.

Alternative Education Schools Are Personal and Focused

Alternative education schools are more personal and focused than conventional ones. Alternative education school students report more personal contacts with teachers and classmates, and observers record more incidents of praise and acknowledgment of students in alternative schools (Young, 1990).

The strengths of the alternative education schools appear to be their well-focused academic programs and their capacity to foster creative human relationships between students and teachers. These exemplary teaching/learning relationships were the result of several features of the schools (Foley, 1983):

- These schools have well-defined student populations, the faculties knew what their students needed, and they planned accordingly.
- Teachers' roles were diversified to allow for increased participation in management and opportunities to counsel students, which enhanced teachers' sensitivity to students' needs.
- A few commonly agreed upon, frequently discussed school rules establish clear standards for conduct. A highly-structured support system enabled students to live within those rules.

Small school size allowed principals and teachers to reach students who were formerly hard to reach in school, as well as encouraged communication and a sense of belonging and limited bureaucratic obstacles.

The Maine Department of Education and the College of the Atlantic conducted a study of seven rural alternative education programs to develop systematic assessment processes for such programs and to provide insight into what qualities contribute to their success (Antonucci & Mooser, 1993). Each program was unique, responding to the needs of its own community. The types of programs ranged from those that provided support within the regular school setting to those that were completely self-contained. The goal of the support centers was to help students experience success in the regular programs. The goals of the self-contained programs were to develop the whole child, foster a sense of belonging, instill a desire to be a productive member of the community, and to complete high school.

Alternative Education Students Feel Valued

An important feature of alternative education is that it gives students at risk a sense of belonging. Few students at risk have successful social lives in the regular schools. Many of the students have a history of dysfunctional relationships with adults. Often their relationships with their alternative-school teachers are the only meaningful adult relationships in their lives. A significant number of these students, in a regular education setting, express feelings of not being valued. Alternative education classrooms, programs, and schools are structured so that students can achieve success and feel valued as individuals, perhaps for the first time in all of their schooling years (Antonucci & Mooser, 1993).

Five Categories of Alternative Education Programs

My review of the available research on alternative education programs lead me to place all of alternative education programs in five distinct categories: Educational Alternative Programs, Teenage Parent Programs, Substance Abuse Programs, Disciplinary Programs, and Youth Services Programs. Educational Alternative Programs are for students who are unmotivated or unsuccessful in the traditional school setting. Students are usually identified as potential dropouts based on criteria such as retention in grade, high absenteeism, failing grades, or low achievement test scores.

Teenage Parent Programs are for students who are pregnant or parenting. The programs offer regular academic classes so students can continue their educational program. They might often provide classes in child growth and development, nutrition and parenting skills. The programs provide auxiliary services designed to meet the special needs of pregnant or parenting students and their children. These services include health services, social services, child care, and transportation.

Substance Abuse Programs meet the special needs of students who have personal or family drug or alcohol-related problems. Students may be served in residential, day treatment, or school-based substance abuse programs. These programs offer educational services while students receive substance abuse treatment or counseling.

Disciplinary Programs provide intervention for students who are disruptive in the regular school environment. These programs provide positive alternatives to out-of-town suspension and expulsion.

Youth Services Programs are for students who are placed in the Department of Juvenile Justice (DJJ), Department of Health and Rehabilitative Services (HRS) or residential or day treatment facilities. Educational services are provided to adjudicated delinquent students in Short-Term Offender Programs (STOP) Camps, halfway houses, detention centers, and Marine Institutes. The programs allow students to continue their education while in special centers. Most of the time, the programs in the five categories employ many of the alternative education strategies in my *List of Research-Based Alternative Education Strategies.*

Chapter 2

TWO INNOVATIVE ALTERNATIVE EDUCATION PROGRAMS

OBJECTIVES

After reading this chapter, teachers should be able to:
- Describe the Truancy Court Conference Program.
- Discuss the terms *mentor* and *mentoring*.
- Tell why mentoring is a proactive and a powerful alternative education strategy.
- Write a minimum of two clear and measurable objectives for a mentoring program.
- Design an organizational chart for a mentoring program at their school.
- Develop a Timetable of Major Milestones for their school's mentoring program.
- List ten community organizations that are potential sources of mentors.
- Explain why some programs do not recruit college mentors under 21 years of age.
- Design a recruiting flyer for the school's mentoring program.
- Design a mentor application for the school's mentoring program.
- Design interview questions for the school's mentoring program.
- Describe some important criteria for matching mentor with protégés.

- Discuss three major community service activities for mentors and protégés.
- Explain process and outcome evaluation relative to a mentoring program.
- Design an organizational chart for a mentoring program.

TWO HELPFUL PROGRAM MODELS FOR K-12 TEACHERS

I have worked with many mentoring programs. Most of the programs were funded through grants from private foundations and local, state, and federal agencies. I sincerely believe it is worth the time and effort for teachers to meet with a district grant writer or a university professor to plan a mentoring program proposal and to submit the proposal to potential funders. Funded programs produce more successes for students and survive for many years. Most unfunded programs do not survive beyond six months and do not serve students well. In fact, they may do more harm than good.

My research and personal experiences reveal that unfunded programs tend to have mentors who do not spend sufficient time with the students and tend to have a high mentor attrition rate. When mentors quit, due to frustration and lack of mentoring program support, after only a few months on the job, students at risk have another of many rejections by adults. Self-esteem is damaged and parents and students are turned off to the idea of mentoring.

In this chapter, I will discuss two funded alternative education programs, the Truancy Court Conference Program (TCCP) and the Mentoring and Tutoring Help (M.A.T.H.) Program. In my discussion, the paramount focus will be on the powerful mentoring component of the M.A.T.H. program. This mentoring component produces substantial successes in our protégés. A significant portion of the M.A.T.H. program can be used by K-12 teachers to establish mentoring programs in their school districts. Both alternative education programs are located in Escambia County, Florida.

Escambia County is recognized as a national leader in the alternative education movement. The University of West Florida (UWF), in Escambia County, is at the forefront of this leadership. Using local practitioners as adjunct professors, UWF offers extensive inservice workshops in alternative education in twenty-two areas such as: anger management, conflict resolution, and technological assistance for students at risk.

UWF has the only master's degree in alternative education in the nation. It offers the only Ed.D. with a specialty in alternative education in the nation. All alternative education initiatives at UWF are a result of a visionary Dean of the College of Education, Dr. Wesley Little. Dr. Little has a profound commitment to alternative education.

Evolution of Truancy Court Conference and Mentoring and Tutoring Help Programs

Historically, Escambia County and the State of Florida have created increased amounts and types of resources for delinquents and their families: more commitment facilities, nonresidential programs, counseling, and other tutorial services. The process for school officials to follow to support a petition for truancy was lengthy, cumbersome, and subjective. Furthermore, since interventions were not accessible through the courts or the Department of Juvenile Justice, (previously a component of the Department of Health and Rehabilitative Services (HRS), the process was simply avoided.

In 1993, the Department of HRS obtained the services of a community service organization to work with truants. Since that time, the procedures for documenting and reporting truancy by the school system have been simplified to encourage the reporting of truancy. The services of the University of West Florida were obtained to coordinate a Mentoring and Tutoring Help (M.A.T.H.) program to work with and to attach to the Truancy Court Conference Program (TCCP). Thus, the Educational Research and Development Center (ERDC) of the College of Education established the M.A.T.H. program with grant awards from the Escambia School District and the International Paper Foundation. The M.A.T.H. program augments and collaborates with the T.C.C.P. (see Figure 1).

Figure 1: TCCP Relationship with M.A.T.H.

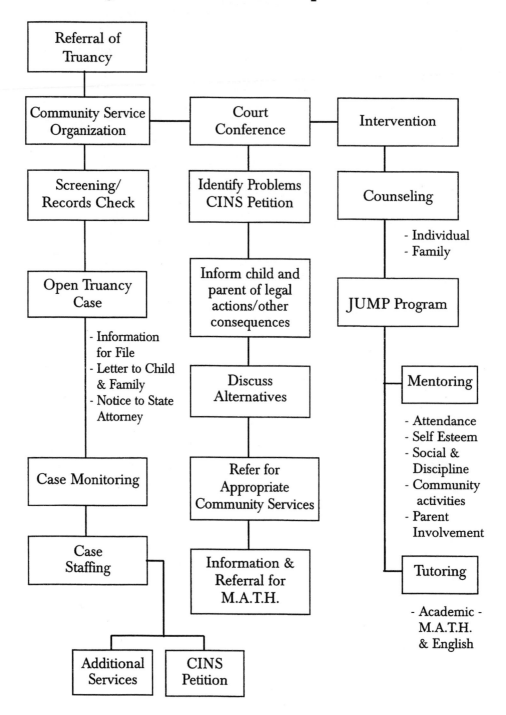

Truancy Court Conference Program

With the inception of the Truancy Court Conference Program came the first system to document, monitor, and process truants. The community service organization in northwest Florida receives truancy referrals from school district visiting teachers (social workers). Each case is evaluated for appropriateness (e.g., age, pending legal actions, etc.) and the students and their families are contacted for services.

Truancy referrals are forwarded to the state's attorney's office. The state's attorney's office sends a letter to parents inviting them to the conference before a judge. This conference is voluntary in nature, both on the part of the students/families and the services provided by the judge (i.e., there is no statutory basis for this court appearance).

The judge attempts to determine the reasons for the truancy, addresses identified problems, offers possible alternative actions, and advises the parent and the student of legal responsibilities and consequences. He encourages the parent and student to participate in counseling with the community service organization.

Following the conference, a counselor from the community service organization meets with the parent and student to explain and offer services. Thereafter, the Truancy Prevention Coordinator monitors the student's school attendance. If the student continues the pattern of frequent absences from school, she/he is considered for case staffing before a committee of professionals from multidisciplinary fields.

At the staffing, information is presented to the committee and the child and parent are given an opportunity to present their circumstances. A decision is made to offer additional services and monitoring, or to recommend a Child in Need of Services (CINS)/Family in Need of Services (FINS) petition to be filed. If a petition is filed, the child and parent are summoned to appear before the court.

The goal of the T.C.C.P. is to avoid further action through improved school attendance. Once in the juvenile system, few resources are available to the student and family, and they are considered low priority in the juvenile justice system. In all likelihood, the truant will need additional services if she/he continues to avoid going to school. The T.C.C.P. is an excellent innovative alternative education program. It is the correct step in the direction of truancy and delinquency prevention.

Mentors Are Effective

It is important for teachers to understand that mentoring is an old idea that works. The word mentor comes from the Greek, meaning steadfast and enduring. The ancient Greek poet, Homer, first coined the word mentor in his epic poem, "The Odyssey." The great warrior Odysseus knew he would be away from home for many years, so he chose a man named Mentor to be the guardian and tutor of his son. Thus, mentor came to mean any trusted counselor or guide.

Mentoring is underutilized as an alternative education strategy (Flaxman, 1992), even though history repeatedly documents that numerous successful people had mentors in their lives. Great athletes point to a coach who encouraged them. "The Greatest," Muhammad Ali, credits his manager, Herbert Muhammad, as being a major reason for his success.

Prominent, political leaders had mentors, too. The Rev. Jesse Jackson, for instance, is one of the many people whose apprenticeship to the Rev. Dr. Martin Luther King, Jr. led to a famous civil rights career. Bona Felisa, the first Alcaldesa (female Mayor) of San Juan, was mentored by Luis Munoz Maris, founder of the Popular Democratic Party in Puerto Rico.

Mentors Are Proactive and Powerful

The importance of a mentor for bonding with the child and facilitating his/her ability to bond with the school and community is unrefuted (Reglin, 1993a). Policymakers, practitioners, and researchers agree that youth need positive, consistent relationships with adults to support their development. A dearth of such relationships in families and institutions of youth at risk has been identified as a factor contributing to young people's difficulties in achieving regular attendance and good grades in school (Reglin, 1990).

According to research, successful mentoring programs have far-reaching benefits, both to the child and the community (Reglin, 1990). As mentors gain greater understanding of issues that schools face, they become powerful forces for involving communities in restructuring schools and enriching the lives of young people.

Mentoring empowers students to succeed in life (Reglin, 1995). No matter how much these students at risk want regular school attendance and good grades, they may not have enough social and personal resources available to achieve these goals. Mentoring is a particularly powerful intervention in the lives of students at risk.

Brendtro, Brokenleg, and Bockern (1991) listed mentoring as an imperative for recessing the high dropout rate among students. In his study of mentoring with disadvantaged youth, Flaxman (1992) concluded that mentoring is a powerful way to provide adult contacts for youth who are isolated from adults in their schools, homes, communities, and work places. And Bernard Lefkowitz, in *Tough Charge: Growing Up on Your Own in America* (1989), found that caring adults were an important factor for the youth who survive the streets and go on to lead successful mainstream lives.

Mentoring and Tutoring Help (M.A.T.H.) Program

Students at risk have become more and more the focus of recent educational reform efforts (Cuban, 1990). The priority for educating these students is higher than ever before. The National Goals for Education and the President's plan for achieving them, "America 2000," reflect widespread agreement that, as a nation, we can no longer be satisfied with educating only a small portion of our population.

At the same time, a consensus about effective strategies for students at risk is emerging. Several recent trends indicate a shift away from traditional remedial programs—that isolate and underestimate the potential of students at risk—to research-based alternative education approaches proven to be effective. An underutilized approach is mentoring. Mentoring gives at-risk youngsters an opportunity to interact with a broader range of children (Johnson & Johnson, 1986; Slavin, 1989).

The Mentoring and Tutoring Help program provides positive role models from the community for the Truancy Court Conference Program students. Involving these students in a personal relationship with the mentor and in school activities with the mentor engenders renewed interest in school and a feeling of belonging. Academic and social life improve with incentives, enhanced self-esteem, and personal attention to specific needs of each student involved.

The M.A.T.H. program assists in finding positive outlets for leisure time and energy which reduce involvement in negative behavior such as gangs, drugs, theft, and idleness. Specific community service projects encourage community involvement and personal responsibility to peers and to the environment.

The M.A.T.H. mentors receive initial training and frequent support refresher training. During the 12-month M.A.T.H. curriculum, mentors visit homes, invite parents to attend small group tutoring sessions as *encouragers,* take students on cultural trips, and take students to sporting activities and to local libraries.

Goal and Objectives of Program

The goal of our Mentoring and Tutoring Help program is to make a positive change in the public school academic success indicators. We seek to reduce truancy, improve academics, make students feel good about themselves, reduce discipline problems, facilitate parental involvement, and facilitate community involvement. To paraphrase, we are committed to reducing the dropout rate in the public schools. The seven objectives of M.A.T.H. are clear, measurable, and obtainable. These objectives are:

(1). One-to-one mentors will be available for M.A.T.H. students each year of the yearly funding period.

(2). Eighty percent of the students will have a 30 percent increase in attendance following program participation compared to their attendance before program participation.

(3). Fifty-one percent of the students will have a one-half letter grade increase in mathematics and English grades following program participation compared to their grade point average before program participation.

(4). Eighty percent of the students will have a 40 percent increase in self-esteem (measured by the Culture-Free-Self-Esteem inventory) following program participation compared to the self-esteem before program participation.

(5). Eighty percent of the students will have 50 percent fewer discipline referrals following program participation compared to the number of discipline referrals before program participation.

(6). Fifty-one percent of the students will attend 30 percent of the M.A.T.H. program scheduled activities. Also, 60 percent of the parents will attend 50 percent more conferences during the year following program participation compared to the year before program participation.

(7). Eighty percent of the students will have a 40 percent increase in involvement in community service projects following program participation compared to the number of involvements before program participation. Also, 80 percent of the students will score 70 percent or greater on a valid and a reliable community service attitude instrument.

Mentors in M.A.T.H.

We contracted with the Escambia School District to provide mentors for one-on-one mentoring and tutors for small group tutoring in mathematics and English. Approximately four to eight students and their families appear at the Truancy Court each month. An analysis of data showed that nearly all of the M.A.T.H. students who have been a member of the M.A.T.H. program for six months or more achieved the program's goal.

Our current mentors and tutors are well-trained. The racial make-up for the M.A.T.H. mentors is 53.3 percent white, 36.7 percent black, 6.6 percent Hispanic, and 3.3 percent American-Indian. The gender makeup is 36.7 percent male and 63.3 percent female.

Protégés in M.A.T.H.

The racial makeup for our protégés is 63.3 percent white, 33.3 percent black, and 3.3 percent Asian-American. The gender makeup is 40.0 percent male and 60.0 percent female. When matching mentor to protégé in the M.A.T.H. program, matching based on race, gender, and culture is an important consideration.

We do not use the word *mentee* because of the negative connotations in mentee. We use the word *protégé*. Dictionaries define a protege as a student under the patronage, protection, or care of someone interested in his career or welfare.

Parents and students sign contracts to be supportive of the M.A.T.H. program. Our students are enrolled in six schools. All six of the M.A.T.H. schools are designated as Chapter I schools. Sixty percent of the M.A.T.H. program students are eligible for Chapter I.

Presently, only one of our schools is a middle school, and the remaining five schools are elementary schools. The M.A.T.H. families are encouraged to attend school functions by the mentors and members of the M.A.T.H. Management Team.

Design

In the initial stage of formulating a mentoring program, it is important for teachers to identify partners. Each partner should have expertise to contribute to the mentoring program. If possible, major partners can commit members to be part of a mentoring program management team or mentoring program advisory council.

My organization, the Educational Research and Development Center (ERDC) of the College of Education, partnered with a community service organization, the Escambia County School District (Office of Alternative Education), the First Judicial Circuit Court of Florida (Juvenile Division), and the Office of the State's Attorney for the First Judicial Circuit Court of Florida. All partners are located in northwest Florida. ERDC provides the mentor program director and the program coordinator. The community service organization and the court provide the assistant directors. The assistant directors have expertise in background screening, training, and other areas. The Office of Alternative Education helps us to obtain funding and facilitates easy access into the schools and easy access to student data such as grades, attendance, and discipline information.

ERDC has a director and 22 staff members. Our M.A.T.H. coordinator oversees the program. The M.A.T.H. coordinator was interviewed, screened and hired by members of the M.A.T.H. Management Team (MMT) (see Figure 2). In our first meeting, we formed the MMT. The ten-member management team includes classroom teachers, parents, a visiting teacher (social worker), and a middle school protégé. The idea of a management team or advisory council is to get representation from all the major players. Members of our MMT are actively involved in every phase of our program. Members of the MMT meet as needed to oversee the M.A.T.H. activities, to plan expenditures, to coordinate the funding, and to coordinate the public relation activities of the program. The M.A.T.H. director devotes a minimum of ten hours per week to the program. Each assistant director devotes a minimum of six hours per week to the program.

Figure 2: M.A.T.H. Organizational Chart

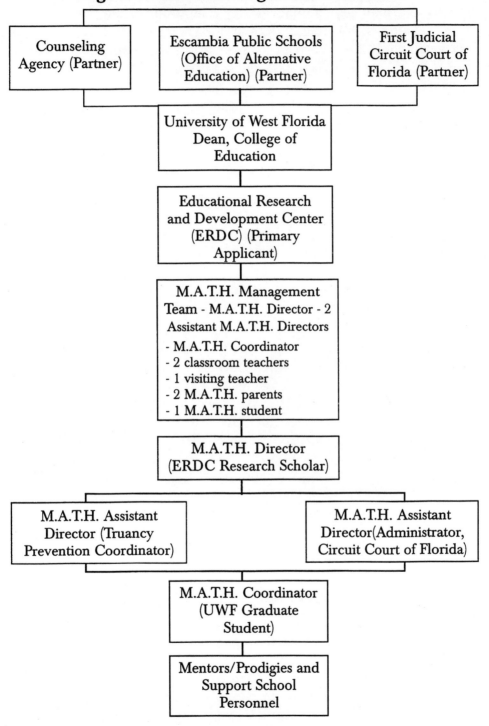

The M.A.T.H. coordinator, assisted by the MMT, organizes, implements, and manages the day- to-day operations of the program. The ERDC staff, visiting teachers, counselors, teachers, and administrators are available to the M.A.T.H. coordinator for assistance. Students in the M.A.T.H. program are referred via the Truancy Court Conference Program. The Truancy Prevention Coordinator, an assistant M.A.T.H. director, schedules the students monthly for a court hearing and works closely with the M.A.T.H. coordinator.

M.A.T.H. student and parent or guardian consent to and enter into a written contract before enrolling a student in the program. Home visits are made for each incoming M.A.T.H. student. Involving the parent and understanding the student's home environment are essential elements of M.A.T.H. M.A.T.H. classroom teachers, visiting teachers, and school administrators are offered training in strategies for teaching at-risk students (see Timetable of Major M.A.T.H. Milestones).

When students leave M.A.T.H., they will be monitored throughout school. We will help them locate tutors and counseling, as needed. When M.A.T.H. students graduate from high school, ability permitting, we will help them obtain college scholarships.

The Escambia public schools supply some classroom space for mentoring, and mentors always have access to ERDC's classrooms. Also, the campus library, and the Parent-Student Center are available for use.

The readers of this text should know, that at the third or fourth planning meeting between teachers and partners, a *Timetable of Major Milestones* needs to be developed. Major events can be planned for each of the twelve months to include hiring a program coordinator, program publicity, recruiting mentors, training mentors, etc. The *Timetable of Major Milestones* is a significant part of any grant proposal to a potential funder. Teachers can use the M.A.T.H. *Timetable of Major Milestones* as a model to develop their timetables.

Timetable of Major M.A.T.H. Milestones

January 1996 through December 1996

January: Hire M.A.T.H. coordinator
                M.A.T.H. and M.A.T.H. Management Team (MMT) put out

memo, flyers, set up TV newspaper, and start radio drive
for mentors

M.A.T.H. coordinator and M.A.T.H. director begin speaking
to service clubs, social clubs, local universities, churches,
and other organizations to attract mentors

M.A.T.H. coordinator works with schools and MMT to
organize mentors and to compile materials

February: Selection and screening of mentors by MMT
Meeting with mentors, teachers, principals, and school liaison
persons for orientation (mentors fill out interest
inventories)
Two-day training session for mentors
M.A.T.H. students meet for explanation of M.A.T.H.
Home visits for protégés who have not had mentor
home visits.
MMT meets with the University of West Florida's Public
Relations office top lan monthly press, radio, and TV
news releases on M.A.T.H. activities

March: Selection of protégés and matching with mentors
Pizza meeting with prospective protégés and their
parents at Parent-Student Center
Meet with protégés for orientation and to fill out interest
inventories
Group pizza party for mentors and protégés to become
acquainted
First individual protÇgÇ/mentor meeting

April: Field trip to Pensacola Beach to see Fort Pickens, the Fort
where Geronimo spent his last days
Return-to-school party after spring break
Meeting with mentors to discuss their needs and problems
and to discuss community service project
Violence prevention activity (Technology with the Internet)

May: Beginning of protégés major community service project
which will continue through summer
Field trip to Sacred Heart Hospital in Pensacola, Florida in
groups
Meeting with mentors to discuss problems and to plan
summer activities
Final mentor protÇgÇ/parent banquet and awards for

attendance and grades
Invitation to protégés/mentors and families to attend
 the three-week Summer
Family Tennis Camp (SFTC)

June/July: Three-week SFTC and fun round robin tennis tournament
Violence prevention activities (anger management, conflict
 resolution, and technology) for protégés, mentors,
 families and teachers at Parent-Student Center
One-day family Zoo activity at Gulf Breeze Zoo for protégés,
 mentors, and families
Help session for major community service project in the
 Parent-Student Center

August 1996 through December 1996

One story a month will appear in newspaper, TV, or radio on some phase or activity of the M.A.T.H. This initiative will be directed by the MMT and the University of West Florida Public Relations Office, in conjunction with the Escambia Public Schools.

August: Concentrated recruitment initiative involving all members of
 the MMT to bring the number of protégés to the required
 level
Selection and screening of additional mentors
Big story in the newspaper's (*The Pensacola News Journal*)
 "Back to School" issue on M.A.T.H.'s old and new
 mentors and protégés
Screening of mentors by MMT
Two-day training retreat for M.A.T.H. returning and new
 mentors at Pensacola Beach

September: Dinner meetings with mentors, teachers, and school
 administrators from each school site (mentors turn in
 interest inventories)
Home visits, selection, and orientation for new protégés (fill
 out interest inventories)
Open hour school day for mentors to become acquainted
 with teachers at mentoring site and after-school pizza
 party for mentors and protégés to get acquainted

October: Field trip to National Naval Museum in Pensacola in groups

Violence prevention activities (parent skills and technology)

M.A.T.H. coordinator meeting with mentors to discuss
problems and to give feedback

Dinner meeting with area employers about time release
for mentors

November: Field trip to Champion International Corporation in
Cantonment, Florida

Meeting with mentors, protégés and parents at the Parent-
Student Center to plan family activities

December: Mentor meeting to discuss possibilities for community
service projects

Christmas party (banquet) for mentors, protégés and parents

Annual mentor two-day training workshop

Assurances from Partners

Evaluation is an important part of any mentoring program. Good
process and outcome evidences of student successes lead to more
funding from funders. It is important for program coordinators to get
written assurances they will have access to student evaluation data.
Gaining access to student data is a problem with most mentoring programs.

We went directly to the superintendent's office to for written assurances. The superintendent's office of the Escambia School District
gave us assurances that they would provide academic records in accor-
dance with their own regulations for use in carrying out the evaluation
of the M.A.T.H. program. All partners gave written assurances that
they would cooperate to the fullest extent possible with the evaluation.

Our additional linkages to M.A.T.H. include the Escambia County
Department of Health, the Escambia County Department of Human
Services, and the Escambia County Sheriff's Department. The
Department of Health and the Department of Human Services are
available for help with health problems, parenting problems, financial
problems, and social services that the mentor cannot handle. The
Escambia County Sheriff's Department and case managers from the
juvenile justice system give seminars to protégés on drug abuse, alcohol abuse, violence, and gangs.

Chapter 3

OTHER COMPONENTS OF THE MENTORING AND TUTORING HELP PROGRAM

OBJECTIVES

After reading this chapter, teachers should be able to:

- Design a recruiting flyer.
- Design a mentor application.
- Write five good interview questions for potential mentors.
- Discuss important considerations in matching mentors and protégés.
- Discuss three community service projects for mentors and protégés.
- Differentiate between process and outcome questions.
- Explain the difference between process and outcome evaluation.
- Design a mentoring program grant proposal using the **20-Step Replicable Model.**

MENTORING AND TUTORING COMPONENTS HELPFUL TO TEACHERS

Components of the Mentoring and Tutoring Help program which help teachers to design mentoring programs for use in their classrooms will be discussed in this chapter. Teachers can read our components

41

and adapt the features of these components to fit their program. For instance, recruiting flyers, mentor applications, and process and outcome questions can readily be adapted by a team of teachers and their partners by modifying our program models in this chapter.

Mentor Recruitment, Screening, and Orientation

Mentor Recruitment

The M.A.T.H. director assembles the M.A.T.H. Management Team (MMT) to handle mentor recruitment. Members of the MMT disseminate memos throughout targeted community organizations outlining the mentor program. They disseminate job descriptions of mentors and brochures explaining how the program will operate. Following the dissemination of memos, MMT members speak to community organizations to explain the need and the role of mentors. MMT members appear on television and community service talk shows to explain the program and to recruit mentors.

Posters and flyers are circulated throughout the community. Church bulletins and radio community service bulletins have notices of mentor recruitment, along with news articles in the local newspaper.

The recruitment efforts concentrate on enlisting mentors who are responsible adults, such as law enforcement officers, military, local service club members, local business persons, and community organization persons. Recruitment is an ongoing process. Some of the organizations we target are listed below.

TARGETED ORGANIZATIONS

- Barber & BeautyShops
- 100 Black Women of Pensacola
- Employment & Training Offices
- Parks Department
- League of Women Voters
- Local Corporations
- Local Religious Institutions
- Parent Teacher Associations
- National Negro Women Organization
- Shriners
- Junior Leagues
- Office of Advocate for the Disabled
- 100 Black Men of Pensacola
- Institutes of Higher Education
- Urban Coalitions
- Urban Leagues
- Local Professional Organizations
- Local Sororities and Fraternities
- Chambers of Commerce
- 4 - H Clubs

We avoid media ads, volunteers off the street, or other random methods. We encourage organizations to recruit their own. For instance, one barber shop recruited other volunteers in the local barber shop network. We are successful when we have the support and commitment from the boss, the top administrator, or commanding officer of the local military base. Their call for volunteers gets results faster than any other system.

We have mixed results with college students as mentors. Reliability is sometimes weak, particularly for the college students under 21 years of age. Reliability is increased with this group with stipends connected to the performance of their duties. In other words, if they do not perform their duties, they do not receive the stipend. Stipends approximate $75 a month and are helpful to offset incidental expenses such as transportation expenses, buying protégés birthday cards, etc.

A very big plus for our recruitment is to assure mentor visitation flexibility. Mentors have their own jobs and need to be able to schedule appointments with protégés as time permits, shifting both day of the week and the hour. While a normal day and hour can be maintained, mentors must have the latitude to change, which does necessitate having a way for mentor and protégé to communicate by phone or via someone at the school or workplace. It is better to shift than to skip weekly appointments.

When possible, we keep mentors from the same organization together when determining matches. This facilitates joint travel, support, and identifying with a school or workplace where mentor visits will occur.

Our "Recruiting Flyer" explains the M.A.T.H program, the support we provide mentors, whom they will work with, and the expectations/commitment. Also, prospective mentors fill out the "Mentor Application" in the Appendix.

Recruiting Flyer

LIKE TO HELP A STRUGGLING STUDENT, RECEIVE MENTORING/TRAINING AND GET PAID A $75 MONTHLY STIPEND

Our Mentor program offers the chance to make a difference in the life of an elementary school or middle school student. Mentors will participate in mentoring training and get feedback on tips to build a good rapport with his/her protégé. Mentors work to improve: academics, self-esteem, behavior, attendance, community service, and parent involvement. The relationship which develops between a mentor and a protégé will provide the kind of support and inspiration missing in the life of the protégé.

Requirements

- Complete an application and an interest inventory.
- Attend training sessions to become familiar with the protégé and to become better prepared to work with the protégé.
- Mentor about two to three hours each week, visit the protégé's home, and phone the parent/parents.
- Maintain a journal reflecting on the mentoring experience with the protégé.
- Phone the coordinator twice each month to update him/her on the protégé.
- Pick up the $75 check each month.

FOR MORE INFORMATION OR TO OBTAIN AN APPLICATION PHONE:

Program coordinator (474-2811) or the school principal or school liaison person (474-2807).

Mentor Screening

The application our mentors complete facilitates background screening and scheduling of training. Applicants indicate three references. References are checked. We consider in a reference check factors such as:

- Emotional maturity
- Job stability
- Quality of family relationships

References must have known the individual for at least one year. One of three references must be the potential mentor's current employer (or supervisor). Other ideal references include next-door neighbors, teachers, fellow employees, or clergy. We do not accept relatives as references.

Interviews are vital parts of our program. Interviews provide us an opportunity to talk with and to observe potential mentors. For them, it is an opportunity to ask questions and to voice any concerns they might have. Some important interview questions we ask are:

Interview Questions

- Why are you interested in becoming a mentor?
- What volunteer experience have you had?
- What should an ideal mentor/protégé relationship include?
- What time commitment could you give to the M.A.T.H. program (hours per week, weeks per year)?
- What preferences do you have for a protégé and why (gender, race, interests)?
- What expectations should you have of your protégé?

At the end of the interview, questions raised by the candidates are addressed. We discuss our process for making a selection decision. We inform the candidates as to how and when they will be notified of the final decision.

If it appears that this individual would be a good mentor, a phone call is made to invite him/her to an orientation workshop. We provide the potential mentor with a local name and phone number to contact for scheduling and assignment. If there are problems or concerns about the individual's ability to serve as a mentor, we tactfully encourage him/her to participate in alternative community service activities.

Mentor Orientation

Prospective mentors attend an orientation workshop detailing the responsibilities and the activities of mentors. Mentors attend a two-day training session at the beginning of the mentoring year. The training session is directed by the M.A.T.H. management team. Mentors receive information as to the mentor expectations, possible activities, planned activities, interest inventories, log sheets for weekly data, student forms, things to avoid, tips for dealing with students at risk, and program evaluation forms.

Matching Mentors and Protégés

All Truancy Court Conference Program (TCCP) students are at high risk. One hundred percent of our Mentoring and Tutoring Help (M.A.T.H.) protégés have multiple risk factors: antisocial behaviors, low academic achievement, poor attendance, potential dropout, substance abuse, emotional problems, as well as gang affiliation. M.A.T.H. protégé selection is based on the program's goals and the immediate and/or long-range need of the child.

Mentors and protégés are matched through an interest inventory (see Appendix) filled out by both. This enables the protégés to be matched with mentors with similar interests in hobbies, work, and community service. It is the responsibility of the M.A.T.H. coordinator to supervise and evaluate the matching of protégés to mentors. We try to culturally match mentors to participating protégés at least 60 percent of the time. We try to gender match mentors to protégés at least 60 percent of the time. Also, recommendations from visiting teachers (social workers) who know protégés are considered, as well as input from family members. As much as possible, our matches consider the needs of the protégé, the mentor expectations, and the level of commitment of the mentor.

Problems common to mentoring programs such as a broken

appointment, lack of transportation, mentor discouragement, and mismatches are dealt with by the MMT, principally the M.A.T.H. coordinator. Teachers and school liaison persons of M.A.T.H. protégés are closely involved with protégés daily by the structure of the M.A.T.H.. Some assist in overseeing M.A.T.H. as a member of the MMT. Most problems are foreseen by the nature of the close association between ERDC partners, teachers, visiting teachers, MMT, and the protégés in M.A.T.H..

Mentor Support and Training

All mentors participate in a comprehensive training program provided by the M.A.T.H. coordinator on campus in the Parent-Student Center and the ERDC's classrooms. The M.A.T.H. coordinator meets weekly with the mentors during the first two months of the program and monthly thereafter to provide support and offer guidance when needed and to ensure ongoing compatibility of the mentor/protégé relationship. The M.A.T.H. coordinator is always available by phone for the mentors. Frequency of contact helps ensure ongoing compatibility of the mentor/student matching, as well as the achievement of the program's goals and objectives.

Mentor/Protégé Activities

In our program, we plan diverse activities. All mentors, protégés, and families are expected to participate in these activities. Below is a listing of some of our activities.

1. Mentors help protégés with personal issues, provide them with general support and guidance, encourage them to stay in school, and dissuade them from participating in delinquent activities.

2. Mentors make home visits to meet with families and to encourage their support of our goals and objectives.

3. Mentors make phone contact with protégés.

4. Mentors get together with protégés individually for lunch, dinner, a show, a walk, to participate in a community service endeavor, etc.

5. Mentors assist protégés with selecting community service projects during visits and participation by family members. Information

and help on the GED, job interview skills, computer literacy, and parenting skills are available. Parents form a parent advisory com the fall and the spring semesters and a major community service activity during the summer. Service activities include working with Habitat for Humanity, planting trees and flowers in local housing projects and trailer parks, helping the elderly in nursing homes, and helping at daycare centers. Mentors work closely with protégés to insure their success in these endeavors.

6. Mentors participate with protégés in violence prevention activities: anger management, conflict resolution, technology, and parent skills training.

7. Mentors participate in and encourage protégés, families, teachers, and school administrators to participate in the M.A.T.H. three-week Summer Family Tennis Camp.

8. Additional mentor responsibilities include mailing the protégé birthday, holiday, or funny cards.

Our violence prevention activities have a significant internet and a role play component. After-school and summer violence prevention activities are held. Each violence prevention activity is about six hours in duration.

In addition to the aforementioned activities, other activities include: training retreat for mentors; award and meet-the-community banquet; return-to-school parties; and field trips to colleges, businesses, industries, and museums. There is one banquet a year for parents, mentors, teachers and students, and community members. Mentors and protégés have a return-to-school party after Christmas holidays and after spring break as an incentive for students to return to school.

In the Summer Family Tennis Camp, we conduct tennis fundamentals, individual tennis instruction, group tennis instruction, and a summer family round-robin tennis tournament. The SFTC is held at the university's tennis courts. Like most universities, our tennis courts are seldom used during the summer and are available for any university program.

The Parent-Student Center is managed by the M.A.T.H. coordinator. We encourage parents to help plan the Parent-Student Center activities.

Evaluation Methods and Processes

Evaluation is critical to assure any mentoring program is operating as designed and is meeting its goals and objectives. Data to be collected for our evaluation is associated with specific program goals and objectives, measures, and data sources. Any mentoring program evaluation designed by K-12 teachers must answer some process and outcome questions:

Process Questions

- What screening mechanisms were used to screen mentors?
- Was the effort made to recruit students at risk adequate?
- Is there a waiting list for students needing matches?
- Is there a waiting list for mentors?
- Was training offered to mentors?
- How many home visits did mentors make, and what activities were they involved in during these visits?
- What types of incentives or rewards were offered to students who demonstrated academic and behavioral improvement during the program year?
- How were parents involved in the program?

Outcome Questions

- How many mentors and protégés were recruited during the program year?
- How many students' behavior got worse, stayed the same, or improved?
- Have student associations with delinquent peers increased, remained the same, or decreased?
- How many mentored students were arrested during the program year, and in how many instances were weapons involved in the commission of acts of delinquency?
- How many students completed the program, and how many left prematurely?

- What was the change in grade-point averages and standardized test scores attributable to the mentoring program?
- What was the change in attendance attributable to the mentoring program?
- What was the change in family involvement in school activities attributable to the mentoring program?
- How many mentors were screened out or dropped out of the program?

After teachers have selected the process and outcome questions for their program, the next step is to rewrite the questions to be objectives. The objectives will be process objectives or outcome objectives. Last, teachers will develop or locate instruments to collect data on each of the objectives. All instruments should be valid and reliable (Reglin, 1993a).

In the M.A.T.H. program, data were collected and analyzed by members of the Math Management Team. We collected data from diverse sources, oftentimes using more than one data collection instrument per process or outcome objective. Additionally, M.A.T.H. mentors have on-going evaluations by the M.A.T.H. coordinator and members of the MMT who meet with them individually during the year. There are additional group mentor meetings. Teachers observe the progress of the protégés and report to the M.A.T.H. coordinator any problems that have arisen or may be foreseen. The M.A.T.H. coordinator meets regularly with protégés to discuss the mentoring process with them.

M.A.T.H. Process Evaluation

1. Mentors maintain a monthly log which includes the number of hours per week with their assigned protégé, mentoring activities, home visits, and phone contacts. These logs are kept on file in the M.A.T.H. office at the end of each month. Data are recorded weekly and evaluated every two months.

2. Parent permission slips are required for each activity the youth participates in with the mentor outside of the school. The permission slips are kept on file at the M.A.T.H. office after the activity is completed.

3. The M.A.T.H. coordinator meets frequently with the mentors and protégés. The meetings facilitate the acquisition of quality information and quality activities for the achievement of goals and objectives. A monthly progress report is completed by the M.A.T.H. coordinator and kept on file.

4. Other data are collected and analyzed from diverse key players using field-tested instruments (see Appendix).

M.A.T.H. Outcome Evaluation

1. The following objective data, based on the program objectives, were collected on our protégés prior to their program participation, at the end of fall semester, at the end of the spring semester, and at the end of the summer session: attendance, grade-point averages, standardized test scores, Culture-Free Self-Esteem inventory scores, discipline referral counts, parent involvement counts, and community service involvement counts. The data were collected on the objectives delineated in Chapter 2.

2. M.A.T.H. is not capable of working with all students. Therefore, students in the Truancy Court Conference Program, not participating in M.A.T.H., serve as the control group. Data were collected and analyzed for these students.

M.A.T.H. Successes

Relative to the seven M.A.T.H. objectives (outcomes) mentioned in Chapter 2, the program achieved objective (outcome) one and 100 percent of our protégés achieved objectives (outcomes) two to seven. Also, the process data, collected and analyzed using the instruments in the Appendix, confirmed an effective program. We presented an analysis of our data to potential funders. The potential funders awarded us additional monies, sufficient to fund more students with one-to-one mentors and to fund more program activities.

Mentoring Model Helpful to Teachers

Chapter Three shares many ideas and procedures helpful to teachers who aspire to establish a research-based mentoring program. The

M.A.T.H. program was established based on research and produced remarkable successes. The **20-Step Replicable Model for Students At Risk** is a summary of the major features of our program. Teachers should study this model carefully and use it as they meet to plan and to develop their mentoring program.

20-Step Replicable Model for Students At Risk

- Coordinate planning meetings with partners.
- Identify possible funding sources.
- Prepare a proposal for a funding source.
- Identify students at risk.
- Get pre and post-test evaluation instruments.
- Develop a policy/procedural manual.
- Hire one project coordinator.
- Publicize the need for mentors and/or tutors.
- Require potential mentors and/or tutors and protégés fill out applications and interest inventories.
- Conduct interviews/background checks.
- Conduct orientation and training.
- Collect pretest evaluation data.
- Match and schedule mentors and/or tutors and protégés.
- Start one-to-one mentoring.
- Start weekly small group tutoring sessions (3 to 4 students).
- Have mentors encourage parents to attend tutoring sessions and school conferences.
- Conduct refresher training for mentors and tutors.
- Collect post test evaluation data.
- Prepare evaluation reports for the funding agency.
- Prepare news releases on the program's successes.

Chapter 4

K-12 TEACHERS GETTING MENTORS INTO THEIR CLASSROOM

OBJECTIVES

After reading this chapter, teachers should be able to:
- Discuss three theories of school achievement.
- Explain why and how to get a mentoring commitment from mentors.
- Write a pledge for mentors.
- Explain why mentors should not play "Fairy Godmother" or "Fairy Godfather."
- Discuss how mentors can facilitate mentor-protégé bonding through the summer.
- State three praising and three listening strategies.
- Explain liability coverage for mentors.
- Write a three-part goal/objectives plan for a protégé.

WHAT TEACHERS SHOULD EMPHASIZE TO MENTORS

K-12 teachers should have high expectations for mentors. Teachers have the responsibility to train and to support mentors throughout the mentoring ordeal. My research and personal experiences show that teachers must support the efforts of mentors to gain knowledge and

53

training in specific areas. These areas are familiarity with theories on school achievement, sincerity about helping, committing for the long-term, bonding, reliability, praising and listening, dos and dont's, terminating if needed, liabilities, communicating with teachers, and setting goals and objectives.

Be Familiar with Theories About School Achievement

Through required reading or a brief lecture, mentors can become familiar with some of the major theories on school achievement. For instance, the Helplessness Hypothesis, the Home Influence Theory, and the Attribution Theory are applicable to school achievement and mentoring programs (Mordkowitz & Ginsburg, 1986).

Helplessness Hypothesis and the Home Influence Theory

The Helplessness Hypothesis states that learned helplessness is a psychological state in which repeated failure to control the outcome of one's situation induces a carryover of passivity and a depressed level of performance to a new situation. The Home Influence Hypothesis suggests that children of parents with high expectations do better than children of parents with low expectations. It takes five variables of home atmosphere into account: (1) family's attitude toward education, (2) reading materials in the home, (3) family stability, (4) aspirations of parents for the child, and (5) extent of cultural activities in which the family participates (Mordkowitz & Ginsburg, 1986).

Attribution Theory

The Attribution Theory (Bruner, 1957) is associated with the investigation of the perception of causality, the judgement of why a particular incident occurred. The degree to which students at risk perceive their own behavior as the controlling factor in receiving rewards or reinforcements is a measure of their internality.

According to the Attribution Theory, internals believe that the reinforcements they received are primarily a result of their own behavior, ability, effort, or characteristics. Yet, individuals, such as students at risk, at the external end of the locus of control continuum, attribute the control of their reinforcements to forces outside themselves: luck, chance, fate, or powerful others (Rotter, 1975). Three areas of causal attributions have been studied: (1) students' own perceptions of certain attributional choices which determine success or failure, (2) attributions due to ethnicity, and (3) attributions due to socioeconomic status combined with ethnic variations.

An example of the first type of attribution study involved a group of high-achieving and low-achieving students who were asked to attribute academic performance to one of the following factors: (1) ability, (2) effort, (3) luck, or (4) ease/difficulty of task. The high-achieving students attributed academic successes and failures primarily to effort, not ability. The low-achieving students believed that ability was, for the most part, the reason for success or failure (Mizokawa, 1988).

Attributions may also be made on the basis of ethnicity or socioeconomic status. In one experimental study, a group of teachers as given pictures of students from different ethnic groups with fictitious data records and as asked to assign grades to the students. The teachers tended to assign higher grades to the Asian-American students (Lehr & Harris, 1994). Asian-American students are stereotyped to be *smarter* than other students.

Overall, the studies which involve causal attributions suggest that most low-achieving students believe ability—an internal, stable, and uncontrollable factor—determines academic success or failure. Most high-achieving students, in contrast, believe that effort—an internal, unstable, and controllable attribute—is responsible for academic success or failure. Also, teachers tend to favor students from high income and ethnic groups known for academic success.

The final perspective found in the review of literature comprises a large number of recent research studies on the effect of cultural influences on the academic success of high-achieving students. According to these studies, parents provide by far the most important cultural influence on students by encouraging them to complete a comprehensive academic curriculum (Barrozo, 1987).

My review of the Attribution Theory leads me to believe that mentors cause more successes for students at risk. Mentoring is more powerful when mentors communicate with parents and work to make parents a significant factor in the mentoring process. As a consequence of the mentoring effect, the students at risk become more internal.

They feel more in control of their destiny, abandon some of the high-risk behaviors, and try to work harder in school.

Be Sincere About Helping Protégés

Not all adults work well with students at risk. This is especially true when these adults are not sincere in their efforts to make a positive difference in the lives of the students. Students at risk are *street smart.* They can readily detect insincere adult mentors.

Sincere adult mentors play a critical role where parents are either unavailable or unable to provide responsible guidance for their children (Floyd, 1993). A survey of 800 career-beginning participants from 16 cities (Harris, 1990) found that at least half of the students said mentoring helped them learn to succeed and to improve their grades. The participants said mentoring helped them avoid drugs, increased their regard for people of other races, and improved their relationships with teachers and family. In addition, the participants reported that mentoring helped them:

- Fulfill their own responsibilities (50%).

- Strengthen family relationships (25%).

- Increase their regard for people of other races (50%).

- Recognize they make a difference (25%).

- Be willing to get involved again (80%).

Who is a mentor? A mentor is a role model, an encouraging person, a friend and confidante, sometimes a cheerleader, and always impartial. A mentor is an advisor first and foremost of a nonjudgmental nature.

My research and experiences reveal that there are two paramount qualifications of a mentor: someone who likes young people, and someone who has the physical and emotional time to spend at least two hours per week engaged with a protégé. The key is a willingness to give a little bit back to the community by being a helping hand to a young person.

Make Long-Term Commitment

Mentors must be asked by teachers, in writing, for a long-term commitment to the mentoring program prior to being matched with a protégé. A mentor should commit, in writing, that he/she will work with the protégé for a minimum of one school year. Much depends on the degree of the bonding of mentor and protégé and the desire of the mentor to facilitate the bonding. Also, some organizations and government agencies authorize employees to use work hours for community services on a limited basis. In Florida, for example, State agencies permit an hour each week of release time per Florida Cabinet resolution. All mentors need to pledge.

Pledge

I understand that the Mentor Program involves spending a minimum of two hours each week with my protégé. I understand that I will attend orientation/training during the year. I will be committing one school year in the program and will then be asked to renew for another year. I have not been convicted within the past 10 years of any felony or misdemeanor classified as an offense against a person or family, of public indecency, or a violation involving a state or federally controlled substance. I am not under current indictment.

To the best of my knowledge and belief, all statements in this profile are true and accurate.

_____

Signature   Date

Facilitate Bonding with Protégé

Mentoring depends primarily on the chemistry between mentor and protégé. While special interests, native language and culture, etc., are helpful, bonding will take place naturally as it would with any two people who meet and become acquainted. The following are *pointers* to facilitate proper bonding:

• Mentor bonding with protégé may take time or be almost immediate. There is no way to guess.

• Patience is a virtue. Mentors should be patient about how long bonding takes. Much depends upon personalities.

• A mentor should not go into the relationship with a protégé with preplanned ideas as to expected outcomes. Prospective mentors need to let nature take its course. Time is an ally.

There are actions which hinder bonding. These hindrances occur when a mentor acts like a:

• Police Officer

• Parent

• Principal

• Psychiatrist

• Teacher

A meaningful relationship with a supportive adult in the elementary and the middle grades offers the protégé someone to whom he or she can turn at times when no other adults are available. Mentors can teach protégés how to obtain help from other helpful adults in their world.

A good mentor-protégé bond is especially helpful at the middle-school level. Middle-school children are still unburdened with the additional academic and social pressures of high school and can utilize the mentoring relationship to help them begin to identify and solidify academic skills and personal goals.

The transition from middle school to high school involves new environments, situations, adults, peers, and expectations. It is at this stressful time that many vulnerable students begin to show a lack of motivation, discipline, and respect for authority in their effort to fit in with their peers. They may begin patterns of truancy and other inappropriate behavior which distances them from school. Students at this stage of development are too often willing to sacrifice personal goals and values in exchange for acceptance by their peers.

A mentor's primary responsibility is to the protÇgÇ, not to his or her family. Mentors are not expected to take on the parental role or undermine parental authority. They are encouraged to meet the student's parents in order to better understand his or her needs. It is okay for mentors to ask the parents what their hopes and dreams are for the child and how mentors can help fulfill those dreams.

Don't Play "Fairy Godmother" or "Godfather"

Mentors should not play "fairy godmother" or "godfather" to the protégé or the family. Gifts are strongly discouraged. If mentors feel they must give some token, the cost should not exceed $2.00. The idea is to not encourage competition among protégés for gifts. There have been instances in other programs where mentors have been *taken* for large sums. Consequently, the mentor-protégé bond was damaged. If a protégé starts asking for gifts, discourage this behavior early.

Keep Communications Confidential

All communications need to be kept strictly confidential. In order to develop the type of bonding in which mentors can be effective, mentors must first be perceived as trustworthy. On log sheets, simply note how the relationship is progressing. For example, "I talked about sports; X seems to be opening up and was responsive to the idea of playing tennis." The only exception to this is if mentors feel that protégés are being physically abused, neglected, or are involved in a life-threatening activity. Report this at once to either the program coordinator, principal, or the school liaison person who will take appropriate action. Mentors are not expected to be social workers.

While mentors may not expose protégés to situations which involve sexual behavior, alcohol, or drug use, they may certainly discuss these issues. Take the position of a caring friend. Mentors should not preach or proselytize no matter what their religious convictions. Let the protege lead the conversation and encourage him or her to think the issue through. Ask questions like: "What do you think would happen?" or "How would this affect your life?" Mentors should share their own experiences, but not try to be a counselor, unless the mentors have been professionally trained.

Facilitate Mentor-protégé Bonding Through Summer

Mentor-student relationships should not end when school closes for the summer. Continue contacts with the protégés over the summer, if possible, using strategies such as the following:

• Give the protégé about six self-addressed and stamped envelopes with instructions to write a note to the mentor at least every other week during the summer.

- Give the protégé a business card and ask him or her to call the mentor weekly during the summer.
- If the protege has a tape player, give him or her a tape of the mentor's favorite music.
- Swap photos with the protégé to serve as a reminder when the mentor is not there.

The importance of a mentor for bonding with the child and facilitating his/her ability to bond with the school and community is unrefuted (Reglin, 1993a).   Policymakers, practitioners, and researchers agree that youth need positive, consistent relationships with adults to support their development. A dearth of such relationships in families and institutions of students at risk has been identified as a factor contributing to young people's difficulties in pursuing a constructive life path.

Be Reliable

Mentors should not forget the date and time of the appointment to see their protégés.

They cannot be late. If there is a need to reschedule, it should be done at the earliest opportunity. Reliability of the mentor will foster the protégé's reliability. To facilitate this effort, a mentor can give his or her protégé an office or home phone number to call if the protégé cannot make the appointment. A business card is helpful and treasured. It will raise the self-esteem of young protégés with peers when these protégés show off the card, and it will be a reminder for the protégés to call. Promises should be kept to protégés. These young people are too familiar with adults who are not consistent in their words or actions. The mentor's role is to demonstrate that adults can and do keep promises.

A second suggestion is to call ahead to see if the protégé is at school or work before leaving to meet the youth. Do not schedule the appointment for first thing in the morning!

In an emergency situation, a mentor can contact the school liaison person, who will relay the message. Another alternative is to find a friend who will stand in for the mentor. Introduce the protégé to this substitute first and involve him or her in at least one prior activity.

If, for any reason, a problem is suspected because of scheduling conflicts, the program coordinator must be notified. He or she will find out if a problem exists and take steps to correct it. Protégés have made a commitment to the program just like the mentors and the program expects them to live up to their agreements.

Deal with Frustrations Caused by Family Members

Sometimes mentors and protégés are frustrated because family plans conflict with a scheduled meeting. Mentors often ask the question, "What if my protege family plans conflict with a meeting we have scheduled?" The answer is that a mentor should complement or add to family opportunities. Time with the mentor is not intended to displace time with the family. Families should continue with normal family plans, including get-togethers, special trips, and vacations. As much as possible, the mentor and the protégé should plan their time together around the normal family schedule. It may be helpful for the program coordinator and the parents to let the mentor and the protégé know about planned family events. Good advance communication will help avoid conflicts.

Another source of mentor-protégé frustration is family members wanting to go with the mentor and protégé on cultural trips or to special events. Mentors are often asked by a family member, "Can I or other family members go on the trip to the museum?" A mentoring relationship is special in part because it is a one-to-one relationship. Even teens who feel very close to their parents sometimes need to talk with friends outside the family. The mentor is an adult friend to the protégé and can talk about things that concern the protégé.

The mentor and protégé have to inform parents about their plans each week. If any family members are uncomfortable with the plans, the plans should be discussed with the family members. Mentors have to be sensitive to family members' concerns and try to find an arrangement that is acceptable to them. Early in the mentoring program, the mentor coordinator should review the **Agreement for Parents of Protégés** with the parents and ask them to sign it. The agreement is proactive and will prevent future frustrations caused by parents.

Agreement for Parents of Protégés

I understand my actions play a major part in my child's relationship with a mentor/tutor. In order to help them I will:

- Give their friendship time to grow, knowing it will not develop overnight.

- Be appreciative of the mentor and show consideration for his/her own busy schedule by being flexible.

- Encourage my child to be considerate of the mentor by having him/her ready on time, or call the mentor if plans need to be changed.

- Have my child properly dressed for each of his/her outings.

- Make arrangements with the mentor if I cannot be home when my child is to return.

- Not deprive my child of the weekly visit with the mentor as a means of discipline. If problems do arise concerning this, I will contact the coordinator.

- Not ask the mentor for favors, as this places him/her in an awkward position.

- Make arrangements for my child to do his/her share in maintaining contact with the mentor.

- Contact the coordinator if there is something about the relationship that concerns me.

_____
        Signature   Date

Practice Good Praising and Listening Strategies

Praise can make a protégé feel wonderful when given in a way that can't be discounted. Find specific occurrences of observable behavior. Don't generalize. For example, "You made an 'A' on that mathematics paper. You really must have studied." Focus on what the protégé can control, not motivations or feelings.

Corrections should gently instruct, not demean a protégé. For example, "You hurt Kedra's feelings when you laughed at her. "Corrections can include the positive and the negative. Give information rather than demand a change in behavior. Put yourself in the protégé's place. How would you like to be treated in this situation? Mentors should be generous with praise and sparing with criticism! Practice good praising and listening strategies.

Praising Strategies

- Catch protégés being good. Comment on some positive behavior demonstrated by the protégés.
- Be sincere. If you cannot be sincere, say nothing!
- Ask protégés about any talent they might have (playing ball, fishing, drawing, etc.). Make a big deal of the talents.
- Show the benefit. How does this effort really help the protégé?
- Ask protégés about their chores at home or their jobs. Praise these successes.
- Ask if you can help. Offer your assistance. Don't order it!
- Praise in public, correct in private.
- Put power into your praise. Positive, proper praising will motivate high performance.
- Listening Strategies
- Don't be too quick to be too judgmental. All protégés are important. All protégés want to succeed.
- Be sincere when listening to the protégés. Maintain direct eye contact. Protégés need the attention of many positive adults.
- Listen for ideas and not just facts. Look for the big meaning in what is said.
- In your conversations with the protégés, let it be known that you care about the protégés' problems, concerns, and obstacles.
- Put what you are hearing into words. After you have listened closely, try to put what the other person is saying and feeling into words and see how they react.
- Use *ice breakers* to make protégés feel comfortable and open up to you. Use the information on the interest inventories.

Be Aware of Dos and Don'ts

Do

- Find out and use the protégé's *nickname* and what he/she likes to do after school as a counseling tool.
- Be real! Show trust, respect, and understanding. An honest relationship will develop.
- With care and understanding, teach, challenge, and support the protégé.
- Share your hobbies, interests, and experiences.
- Be a friend!
- Have high expectations for the protégé; communicate feedback to the program coordinator and teachers.
- Help the program coordinator locate more outstanding mentors/ tutors (the more mentors, the better we can help protégés).

Don't

- Attempt to replace the parents in situations that the parents should handle or the teachers in situations the teachers should handle.
- Take the side of the protégé when the protégé is trying to play you against the parent or teacher.
- Lose or misplace your integrity by trying too hard to facilitate the relationship.
- Lose your patience and become pessimistic.
- Tell the protege to *do it this way* because I did it like that at your age.
- Represent yourself as an authority figure.
- Expect overnight, huge changes in academics, self-esteem, and behavior.
- Patronize.
- Be insincere.

Know When to Terminate

Mentors are not effective when they are not compatible with their protégés. Unfortunately, not all matches are on target. If after three visits with a protégé there seems to be a conflict, it may be necessary to find a different protege or terminate.

It must be understood that the relationship will take time to establish. A mentor experiencing discomfort with a protege should contact the program coordinator or the school contact person as early as possible. They may be able to help. If not, other arrangements will be made.

If a mentor decides to leave the program because circumstances beyond the program's control make it impossible for the mentor to meet commitments, another mentor will be sought for the protégé. The program coordinator will ask the departing mentor for help in finding another mentor for the protégé. He or she will ask the departing mentor to help the protégé recognize that his/her leaving has nothing to do with the program or the protégé. Sometimes young people negatively internalize unrealistic messages. Mentor programs should avoid this.

Know About Liability Coverage

Mentors who take their students off school grounds on occasion must obtain the permission and approval of the principal. When they do this, a field-trip form must be signed by all parties to cover liability. Most school systems have coverage for volunteers who perform duties at school or accompany students on field trips. Ask the principal or an assistant principal if there is any doubt.

Mentors should have a driver affidavit on file in the school office that includes proof of current automobile insurance. Mentors only have car insurance if and when an occasion arises where they will be using their personal vehicles to transport protégés to an activity or site visit. Regularly scheduled meetings which take place at school or in the workplace are usually the liability responsibility of the site.

Communicate with Teachers

Communication is important to the success of this program. Protégés' teachers can communicate frequently with the mentors by telephone, notes, or in person. Teacher-mentor sessions can take just five minutes, or they might be scheduled for an entire faculty meeting. Whatever the length of time, mentors benefit from talking to teachers and support staff; they learn many strategies for improving their students' attitude, behavior, and self-esteem.

In addition, school psychologists, social workers, and guidance counselors provide useful information about each student on a regular basis.

Throughout the year, mentors can offer strategies that have worked for them. These can be compiled monthly by the program coordinator and shared with all through a newsletter or e-mail. The newsletter or e-mail serves to notify mentors of upcoming events, vacation schedules, summaries of research in the field, and results of yearly evaluations.

Set Goals and Objectives with Protégés

First, I will define a goal. *A goal is something a mentor wants to accomplish. A goal is something to aim towards.* Choices become clearer when you know what you are after. Goals should be realistic and manageable. Objectives come from goals. Objectives can be reached quickly to provide small successes, which multiply and encourage protégés to work towards the larger goals. The mentor and protege should work together to set realistic goals and objectives for the protégé .

Objectives should be short-term, with manageable tasks to be completed during the semester that the mentor and protégé meet. Obstacles will surface, but instead of giving up, look for possible solutions. Mentors are there to help protégés overcome the obstacles and to assist them in building a network of support within their school. Guidelines for setting goals and objectives are:

- Importance–A goal must be something that really needs to be done.
- State clearly–Know exactly what should be achieved.
- Realistic–Be realistic in terms of the time and energy you have.

- Control—Plan goals and objectives that are feasible to do.
- Measure—Set time limits and levels of achievement.

Goals and objectives must be *do-able*. They should be something that can be achieved within the fall or spring semester. If goals and objectives are stated clearly, one will know when the goals and objectives have been achieved. Below is a model three-part goal/objectives plan. (The I represents the protégé).

Goal:	I will improve my mathematics grade this term.
Objective:	I will have at least a one-half letter grade increase in my mathematics grade at the end of the term.
Protégé Activity:	I will do my mathematics homework three times a week.
Joint Activity:	We will review together before a test.
	We will attend the protégé's mathematics class.
	We will find a mathematics tutor for the protégé at his/her school, the nearby college, or the nearby community center.

Note that the goal is set for success; it doesn't indicate the protégé will get 100 percent on a test or an A+. It is also based on the knowledge that this is something the protégé really wants and needs to do. Helping the protégé achieve a single limited goal can lead to the habit of setting goals to obtain even greater results—finishing high school and going to vocational school.

Chapter 5

TIPS TEACHERS CAN USE TO BUILD MENTORING PROGRAMS

OBJECTIVES

After reading this chapter, teachers should be able to:
- Describe three successful mentoring programs.
- Design a *Student at Risk Referral/Profile of a Student at Risk* instrument for your school.
- Explain the importance of a school contact person or a school liaison person.
- Write a mission statement for a mentoring program.
- Write goals and objectives for a mentoring program.
- Explain how to facilitate family involvement in the mentoring program.

Partnering with university professors or the school district research office, K-12 teachers can be proactive and take the lead in bringing research-based mentoring programs into their classrooms. No longer can one teacher be expected to work alone with a class having a significant number of students at risk. More adults are needed to give additional individual attention to the myriad and diverse needs of students at risk. Mentoring can be done before class, in class, or after class.

My research and personal experiences show there are specific areas teachers must have knowledge in to facilitate building effective mentoring programs. The areas are familiarity with effective mentoring programs; identifying protégés and school liaison persons; writing

69

mission statements, goals, and objectives; and being aware of the changed family structure and being a facilitator of family involvement. Briefly, I will address the areas.

Familiarity with Effective Mentoring Programs

There are five major help areas which underlie effective mentor programs. These areas are to help students at risk:

- Help themselves
- Set realistic goals and objectives, and plan for the future
- Practice good citizenship
- See the connection between their education and the world of work
- With personal issues, family problems, and girlfriend/ boyfriend problems

Below is a summary of nine effective mentoring programs which have the five areas as their foundation.

Campus Partners in Learning

Campus Partners in Learning (CPIL) encourages college and university students to act as mentors to middle-school youth who are at risk of not completing a secondary education or making the transition to productive adulthood (Education Commission of the States, 1989). This national project, comprised of 202 colleges, offers information, technical assistance, and national visibility for campus-based mentoring initiatives. CPIL is part of Campus Compact, a project of the Education Commission of the States (ECS) that promotes mentoring as an effective intervention strategy for students at risk. The most successful programs include the following components: (1) collaboration and communication between local or state agencies, higher education institutions, and public schools; (2) the financial and administrative support of the participating college or university; (3) comprehensive training and support for participating college students, including opportunities for reflection; and (4) program goals that include personal as well as academic growth for students at risk.

Rendering Educational Assistance through Caring Hands (REACH)

A mentoring program, Rendering Educational Assistance through Caring Hands (REACH), was implemented at Langston Hughes Intermediate School in Reston, Virginia, during the 1988-1989 school year (Blum & Jones, 1993). The program components include a peer support group that meets once a week and daily, one-on-one contacts between students and their adult mentors.

The teachers who teach the students in the REACH program indicate that the students improve in promptness to class, preparation for class, quantity of daily assignments completed, participation in class, classroom behavior, positive interaction with peers, and report card grades. A comparison of the third-quarter and first-quarter grades in mathematics, English, science and social studies of the students in the REACH program showed the following (Blum & Jones, 1993):

- 52 percent reduction of Fs
- 10 percent reduction of Ds and D+s
- 16 percent increase of Cs and C+s
- 22 percent increase in Bs and B+s

Big Brothers/Big Sisters

One of the oldest organizations that offers mentoring is Big Brothers/Big Sisters. For the past 88 years, it has recruited adults and has provided them with extensive training to serve as role models for children and youth. This organization is recognized as one of the better mentoring organizations. There are numerous branches throughout the nation. Consistently, Big Brothers/Big sisters has made a significant difference in the lives of students at risk.

IBM's Corporate Mentorship Program

IBM's corporate mentorship program, in Nashville, Tennessee, is for students with special needs and restrictive work schedules. The mentors serve as counselors who encourage, motivate, and advise the students. The students are enrolled at the Cohn Adult Learning Center, an accredited high school for educationally disadvantaged adults who did not graduate from high school.

Recruiting Flyer

LIKE TO HELP A STRUGGLING STUDENT, RECEIVE MENTORING/TRAINING AND GET PAID A $75 MONTHLY STIPEND

Our Mentor program offers the chance to make a difference in the life of an elementary school or middle school student. Mentors will participate in mentoring training and get feedback on tips to build a good rapport with his/her protégé. Mentors work to improve: academics, self-esteem, behavior, attendance, community service, and parent involvement. The relationship which develops between a mentor and a protégé will provide the kind of support and inspiration missing in the life of the protégé.

Requirements

- Complete an application and an interest inventory.
- Attend training sessions to become familiar with the protégé and to become better prepared to work with the protégé.
- Mentor about two to three hours each week, visit the protégé's home, and phone the parent/parents.
- Maintain a journal reflecting on the mentoring experience with the protégé.
- Phone the coordinator twice each month to update him/her on the protégé.
- Pick up the $75 check each month.

FOR MORE INFORMATION OR TO OBTAIN AN APPLICATION PHONE:

Program coordinator (474-2811) or the school principal or school liaison person (474-2807).

Castlemont High School Mentor Program

At Casetlemont High School, in Oakland, California, a mentor program was established by high school alumni who share their experiences with Castlemont students. The mentors include a professional ball player, politicians, police chief, fire captain, attorneys, business people, dentists, and artists. The program emphasizes orientation to the mentors' professions.

Mentors, Inc. in Washington, D.C.

Mentors, Inc., in Washington, D.C., recruits mentors from law firms, corporations, and universities. They provide students with a mentor for all three high school years. Most of the students selected for the program are not in danger of dropping out but are at risk of not achieving to their potential. Mentors, Inc. improves their school performance and focuses students' career plans.

Project RAISE

Project RAISE (Raising Ambition Instills Self-Esteem), in Baltimore is a group of sponsoring organizations ranging from churches to banks. Each adopts a class of sixth-graders and provides mentors through high school graduation. The mentors commit to at least one year of weekly contacts, including one-on-one contact twice a month. RAISE II adopts students in the second grade and offers them mentors through the start of high school.

Mentors for African-American Students

Mentors for African-American Students is a mentoring program designed to improve the academic achievement of black, male, urban, high-school students (Laughrey, 1990). The program utilizes black adult mentors from both the community and the school's faculty. Mentors function as role models, advisers, and resource persons.

The program design includes the following components: (1) a school-based committee responsible for program implementation and for identifying student participants, (2) training for mentors, (3) periodic progress reports prepared by mentors, (4) after-school tutoring, (5) small group counseling, (6) career planning, and (7) program evaluation based on improvement in student test scores. Most of the program is funded from the regular school budget, with supplementary funds provided by the Parent Teachers Association. Participants show improvement in attendance, test results, and postgraduation planning.

Black Male Youth Enhancement Program

Some mentor efforts are culture-specific. One example is the Black Male Youth Enhancement Program at the Shiloh Baptist Church in Washington, D.C. It offers a comprehensive year-round program of cultural, educational, and spiritual activities serving at-risk boys, ages 9 through 16. It includes a daily after-school study hall and weekly group meetings with mentors to discuss critical concerns in these boys' lives.

Know How to Identify Protégés

There exist myriad and diverse procedures for identifying protégés. Teachers can fill out a *Request Form* for each student they think would benefit from having a mentor. They can record relevant information about the student's family background, personal interests and hobbies, as well as reasons why the student would benefit from the mentoring experience and strategies mentors might use to assist their student. Since there are many more students needing mentors than there are available mentors, it might be necessary to establish selection criteria. Priority can be given to those students who exhibit one or more of the following characteristics:

- One-parent family with little or no support
- No parents, being raised by someone else with little or no support
- Intact family with history of drug or alcohol abuse
- Poor attendance at school
- Increased hostility
- Frequent trips to the principal's office
- Increased detentions
- Poor attitude

- Lack of self-esteem
- Inability to take risks
- Poor eye contact

Protégés may be referred by teachers, guidance counselors, social workers, the court system or their parents. I recommend teachers use the **Student at Risk Referral/ Profile of a Student At Risk** forms to identify these students. After students are identified for the mentoring programs, teachers can mail a copy of the **Parent Information and Consent** form for parents to complete, sign, and return to the mentoring program coordinator.

Student At Risk Referral

Student _____

Teacher _____

1. Attitude in general that causes concern.

2. General comments about grades.

3. Absences.

4. Social observations.

5. Personality description.

6. In your opinion, does this student lack academic focus?

7. In your opinion, does this student need friends?

8. In your opinion, is this student a potential dropout?

9. In your opinion, could this student benefit from a mentor?

Profile of a Student At Risk

10. Single parent family
11. Low academic motivation
12. Limited view of the future
13. Below grade level in reading, writing and mathematics skills
14. Low self-esteem
15. Influenced by peers more than parents or family members
16. Do not trust adults
17. Perceive many adults as being *phonies*
18. Unable to cope adequately with family problems
19. External locus of control (no control over successes)

Parent Information and Consent

I. Parent Information Section

Dear Parent:

During the 1997/1998 school year, our students have a unique opportunity to work with adult mentors. Mentors work to improve attendance, academics, self-esteem, behavior, parent involvement, and community involvement.

Mentors will:

- Mentor a minimum of two hours each week
- Visit the student's home and phone the student and parent frequently
- Meet with the program coordinator monthly about his/her protégé

As a parent, we ask you to support the program by agreeing to:

- Be knowledgeable about the mentoring program
- Ask your child about his/her conversations and the relationship with the mentor
- Communicate with the coordinator, principal, or school liaison person on concerns you have regarding the program or your child's relationship with the mentor
- Visit the school and meet the coordinator and mentor whenever your schedule permits

Your signature indicates your agreement to the above and permission for your child's participation. Please have your child return this signed letter to the school counselor.

| _____ | _____ |
| Protégé Name | Parent/Guardian Signature |

Address: _____　　Phone: _____

_____　　Date: _____

II. Parent Consent Section

I, _____ , the parent/guardian of _____ , permit him/her to participate in the mentor program. I understand that failure to abide by the rules and regulations of the program and to make a commitment to the program will be just cause for immediate dismissal from the program.

I understand that personal liability while in the program is the responsibility of the Protégé and the parent.

Date _____

Protégé_____　　Parent/Guardian _____

Program
Coordinator _____

Mentor
Assignment _____

Participation by students works best, in most cases, when it is voluntary. Students who are receptive to new ideas, committed, have the ability to listen and ask questions, and show enthusiasm will profit most from the experience.

The mentor program can have many categories of students in at-risk situations or a particular population, such as all seventh-grade students. It can concentrate on academic skills, truancy, delinquency, career awareness, or social skills. The focus of a program is determined by the needs of the protégés to be served. Each school and community has unique problems which must be considered when developing a mentoring program.

Know How to Identify School Liaison Persons

At each school site, all administrative details relating to the mentor program need to rest with one individual. Some principals prefer to do this, but in most cases, the school counselor, administrative aide, or social worker assumes the liaison role. In some cases, teacher aides are the link to the company or organization that is providing mentors. Also, each company or organization providing mentors must designate one person as liaison. This person is usually someone from the Personnel or Human Resources Department and does not have to be a mentor. The liaisons play a critical role in matching mentors and students, arranging for a replacement of mentors, conducting evaluations, coordinating year-end celebrations, and scheduling teacher/mentor/parent meetings and other functions.

Write Mission Statements

A mission statement is a broad, one-sentence statement revealing the general purpose of the mentoring program. A mission statement is written for teachers to use as a model to develop their mission statements.

The Santa Rosa Mentoring Program links eleven- and twelve-year-old male alternative school students in a rural county with corporate executives who provide consistent guidance and help on a one-to-one basis to encourage protégés to improve their grades and to curtail discipline problems.

Uses for the mission statement
- Newspaper, radio, magazine, newsletter, and radio public relations
- Fund raising
- Communicating with community, church, military, and business organizations
- Internal operations

The mission statement should answer most of these questions and should be stated very simply:
- What does the program want to accomplish?
- How does the program plan to accomplish this task?
- Who is the target population (by age, gender, geography, income, etc.)?

Evaluate the mission statement by answering these questions:
- Is it realistic?
- Is it ambiguous?
- Does it reflect the mentoring program organizers' values and beliefs?
- Does it reflect the students' at risk needs?
- Will it capture the attention of the mission statement readers?

Write Goals

Goals come from the mission statement. Goals are statements on which specific objectives are built. Goals will take into account the information you learn from your needs assessment, the philosophy of your organization, the people involved, your resources, etc. Based on the mission statement above, two goals might be:
- To help students increase their grade point average in mathematics and English
- To help students reduce their discipline referrals

Write Measurable Objectives

Objectives come from goals. Objectives are specific, measurable activities: the *who, what, when, where, etc.,* of the program. Continuing with our example, objectives could include:

- Having 51 percent of the students with a one-half letter grade increase in mathematics and English grades following program participation compared with their grade point average before program participation
- Having 80 percent of the students with 50 percent fewer discipline referrals following program participation compared with the number of discipline referrals before program participation

Some important considerations are :

- When deciding on the goals and objectives of your mentoring program, please be realistic. Mentoring can't do everything.
- The program needs to have a significant connection with other aspects of the students' lives, family, part-time jobs, child care responsibilities, etc.
- Develop short and long-term objectives; students will have different needs at different times.

Meeting short-term objectives gives mentors and students a feeling of success early. This feeling helps keep enthusiasm and involvement high, reduces attrition, and focuses the work of mentor and student.

To teachers considering implementing a mentoring program, Hamilton and Hamilton (1992) offer recommendations derived from experience gained by Cornell University's Department of Family Studies in a demonstration mentoring program called *Linking Up*. The recommendations include the following:

- Employers and organizations that are willing to take on the task of finding volunteers within their ranks are a more promising source of mentors than one-at-a-time recruitment.
- Mentors need continuing support. Even mentors who appear to be successful express frustration about the need for additional support beyond the initial orientation and training.

Awareness of Changed Family Structure of Students

The changing family structure is causing alarmingly high school dropout rates and a disturbing increase in violent crime by juveniles (Reglin, 1993b). Bountiful babyboomers, now in the peak of their careers, make competing in the workforce exceedingly difficult for the young, the uneducated, and the inexperienced. More and more children are returning home as adults, unable to support themselves. Even military service, once a last resort for some young people, can now selectively eliminate those without high school diplomas or with criminal records.

The disintegration of the family is predicted to continue, with the result being more children in single parent homes and a higher dropout rate in the public schools. Few would dispute that many unfortunate circumstances have converged to weaken the family: mothers forced into the workplace for economic reason; a decline in parental responsibility for child support and childrearing; increasing numbers of teen pregnancies and children born out of wedlock; high divorce rates, as well as declining marriage rates; increased child abuse and neglect.

In general, there are ever-increasing numbers of children being raised in poorly-educated, single-parent families who live in poverty, while the extended family support systems erode (Reglin, 1993a). Few fathers are in the home and children, particularly minority male children, seldom see positive role models and positive mentors. There is a lack of community networking, familiar human relationships, and cultural guidance for the young people. The burden of children's socialization falls solely on these parents. Parents and protégés need help with this burden. This need for help justifies the need for effective mentoring programs.

Facilitator of Family Involvement in Mentoring Program

Involvement of the family is a vital component of the school or any program seeking to help students. Families must be encouraged to participate. Creative strategies can be employed to get them involved (Reglin, 1992b).

The Norwalk Mentoring Program has a creative approach to family involvement. In this program, the school district conducts a workshop series in the evenings for parents and mentors. Babysitting and taxi fares, if needed, are paid through mini-grants provided by some of the companies involved in the program. Many of these parents had never come to school for parent meetings or teacher conferences. Data on parent involvement during the first years of the program indicate that 63 percent attended the parent-mentor evening workshop series on a regular basis, and 72 percent attended the spring parent-teacher conference. This data bode well for the future success of the program. The workshops are led by professionals who are experts in their field. Recent workshop topics include *Stress in the 90's, AIDS Prevention, How to Listen to Your Child, How to Bridge the Communication Gap Between the Child and the Adult, Drug and Alcohol Abuse,* and *How to Read to Your Child.*

Each parent of a student in the mentoring program is sent an invitation before each workshop. One social worker entices parents to her workshop with these warm words: "It will give you a chance to meet your child's mentor, taste delicious home-baked desserts and enjoy a fun-filled evening. It is really important for you to come." The invitation is always followed up with personal telephone calls.

CONCLUSION

Opportunities for mentoring programs are excellent. In many states, there is a significant talented, retired senior citizen population that can serve as mentors. Many public schools are in close proximity to universities, military bases, large corporations, community organizations, and churches. These are good sources of mentors. Research shows that mentors increase students at risk academic success factors. Many private foundations and government agencies are awarding grants and contracts to fund solid mentoring programs.

As I have informed teachers, a mentoring program will not serve students well if it is a "quick fix" program. I refuse to help establish a "quick fix" program. The life of the program is too short, and the program will frustrate mentors, protégés, parents, teachers, and school administrators. Mentors will quit working with the program due to high levels of frustration and subpar program support. Students at risk will experience another rejection by adults, damaging their self-esteem. Furthermore, teachers and school administrators become turned off to mentoring as an effective alternative education strategy.

My research reveals that the number of students at risk is increasing. Why? The public system, in its traditional way of doing business, is failing our children. The burden of the student at risk is overwhelming. The number of single parent families, where the father is absent from the household, is increasing. Students at risk are turning away from school and turning to truancy, delinquency, pregnancy, gangs, and crime. Therefore, mentors are needed, more than ever, to help in these at-risk situations.

More schools are participating in school-based management wherein teachers are key players in major school decisions, including how school funds are spent and what kind of programs should be housed at the schools. Teachers can bring more mentors into the classroom and into the school to give students at risk additional one-on-one help.

The one-on-one help is important due to the excess baggage students bring into the school from the home, community, peers, television, radio, video games, and the Internet. Our students sorely need the extra help and encouragement. Daily, they are confronted with negative behaviors which undermine the good values taught in the schools and in some homes.

Now is the time for teachers to be proactive. Teachers must innovate ideas and seek money and programs to support the ideas. *Mentoring Students At Risk* facilitates this effort. It also helps teachers to understand how to design, fund, operate, and evaluate a research-based mentoring program, as well as assists coordinators of church and community-based mentoring programs.

Mentoring Students At Risk prepares K-12 teachers to pursue mini-grants or to pursue major grants in collaboration with the university, school district, or community expertise. The major grants might come from the local school board, private foundations, state agencies, or federal agencies. The grants will support a research-based mentoring program and contribute to developing positive academic success indicators for students at risk. With an influx of grant awards and community support, mentoring programs shall exist for many years and shall serve students well. Teachers know that the argument for restructuring rests, for the most part, on the fact that America's schools have reached a point where minor changes or improvements to the current system will be inadequate.

This book advocates alternative education as a significant restructuring solution for education. Mentoring students at risk is a powerful and an effective alternative education strategy. Thus, the book will support the efforts of K-12 teachers to establish research-based mentoring programs in their schools. These mentoring programs will facilitate the academic successes of students.

APPENDIX

MENTOR APPLICATION

Name_____

Check one:
❑ Graduate student   ❑ Faculty/staff
❑ Community member who is not a university

Business address (if employed) _____
_____

Phone number_____   Best time to call _____
Home address _____
_____

Educational background _____

List previous work or experience with adolescents 6 to 15 years of age (community basketball, church, tutoring, etc.). _____
_____
_____

Would you prefer to be paired with a male student or a female student? Circle one.
                     Male   Female

List three references who have known you for at least one year. Relatives are not acceptable. (By supplying this information you are granting us permission to contact the references listed).

References' name, address, and phone number

_____
_____
_____

When, during the week, can you attend a two-orientation session? (List two days and two time blocks). Training is held at the university Parent-Student Center.

_____
_____

INTEREST INVENTORY

1. If you could plan a perfect day in your own town, what would you plan to do?

2. What kind of music do you like?

3. If you could learn to do one thing perfectly - with no effort - what would you choose to learn?

4. What is your favorite TV show?

5. What do you enjoy doing for fun?

6. What is the thing you like best about yourself?

7. Describe what you like to do on the weekends?

8. If you could meet anybody in the world, who would you meet and why?

9. If you could visit any place in the world, where would you go and what would you do there?

10. Do you speak a foreign language? If yes, which one?

11. What are your favorite sports?

12. Are you artistic at all? Please explain.

SELECTED EVALUATION FORMS

Public School District Consent Form for Mutual Exchange of Information

Student's Name _____

DOB _____   School _____

SSN# _____   Date_____

    I hereby authorize the mutual exchange of records regarding the above named student between the public school system and the following agencies that are listed below. I also understand that all information will be confidential and will be used only for the purpose of aiding my child. To facilitate ongoing processes, this authorization shall be in effect from the date signed below through exiting the public school system.

The following information and records may be released:

- Psychological Tests   • Social/Development History
- Individual Educational Plans   • School Records
- Other information and records that are significant to my child

Agencies Authorized to Exchange information

- Public School District
- University

    I hereby certify that I am the parent or legal guardian of the child named above, or that I am a student of majority age and have authority to sign this release.

Signature _____   Date _____

Address _____

City/State/Zip Code _____

MENTORS' EVALUATION OF
MENTORING PROGRAM

Using the following scale, rate the items:
0-None, 1-Poor, 2-Okay, 3-Satisfactory, 4-Good, 5-Outstanding.

_____ My student showed improvement in study habits.

_____ My student showed increased interest in good grades.

_____ My student improved in his/her grades.

_____ My student had good school attendance.

_____ My student has a better attitude about school.

_____ My student became involved in some school activities.

_____ My student showed an improved attitude about himself
and about his/her capabilities.

_____ My student does not give up as easily as he once did.

_____ My student learned how to set goals and reach them.

Write short answers.

1. What is the major problem you observed with this program?

2. What are your suggestions for improving the program next year?

3. What advantages of the program would make it worth
continuing?

4. Are there any personal benefits that you have gained?

PROTÉGÉS' EVALUATION OF
MENTORING PROGRAM

Use rating numbers according to the scale:
0-None, 1-Poor, 2-Okay, 3-Satisfactory, 4-Good, 5-Outstanding.

_____ I improved in my study habits.

_____ I improved my grades overall.

_____ I have more interest in, and take more responsibility for, making good grades.

_____ My school attendance improved.

_____ My attitude toward school and education improved.

_____ I have a better attitude about myself.

_____ I feel capable of controlling my grades and school success.

_____ I learned something about making friends.

_____ I choose to get involved in extracurricular activities.

_____ I do not give up as easily as I once did.

_____ I learned to set goals and to plan to reach them.

Write short answers.

1. List one (or more) problems of the mentoring program.

2. Give at least one suggestion for improvement of the program.

3. What major advantage of the program makes it worth continuing?

REFERENCES

Antonucci, F. J., Jr., & Mooser, E. (1993). *Research report: Assessment of alternative Programs.* Augusta, ME: Department of Education.

Barrozo, A.C. (1987). *The status of instructional provisions for Asian ethnic minorities: Lessons from the California experience.* Paper presented at the Annual Meeting of the American Educational Research Association.

Beck, M.S. (1991). *Increasing school completion: Strategies that work.* Monographs in Education. Vol. 13, C. T. Holmes (Ed.). Athens, GA: College of Education, University of Georgia.

Bendtro, L.K., Brokenleg, M., & Bockern, S.V. (1991). *Reclaiming youth at risk: Our hope for the future.* Bloomington, IN: National Educational Service.

Blum, D. J., & Jones, L. A. (1993). On the scene: Academic growth group and mentoring program for potential dropouts. *The School Counselor,* 40, 210-211.

Bruner, J. S. (1957). On perceptual readiness. *Psychological Review,* 64, 123-128.

Bucci, J.A., & Reitzammer, A.F. (1992). Teachers make the critical difference in dropout prevention. *The Educational Forum,* 57, 63-69.

Chalker, S.C. (1996). *Effective alternative education programs: Best practices from planning and evaluating.* Lancaster, PA: Technomic.

Congressional Oversight Hearing on Local Gang Diversion Programs (1993). Serial No. 103-19. Washington, D.C.: U.S. Government Printing Office.

Conly, C.A. (1993). *Street gangs: Current knowledge and strategies.* U.S. Department of Justice, Office of Justice Programs, National Institute of Justice. Washington, D.C.: U.S. Government Printing Office.

Cuban, L. (1990). At-risk students: What teachers and principals can do? *Educational Leadership,* 46(5) 29-32.

Duttweiler, P.C. (1995). *Effective strategies for students in at-risk situations.* Bloomington, IN: National Educational Service.

Duttweiler, P.C. (1994). Is school reform serving the at-risk population? *Journal of At-Risk Issues,* 1(2), 3-12.

Education Commission of the States (1989). *At-risk youth and the role of college and university students.* ERIC Reproduction Service, ED No. 315463.

Finn, J. D. (1991). Measuring Participation Among Elementary Grade Students. *Educational and Psychological Measurement,* 5(2), 393-402.

Fiske, J. (1991). For cultural Interpretation: A study of the culture of Homelessness. *Critical Studies in Mass Communication,* 8(4) 455-74.

Flaxman, E. (1992). *Mentoring in action: The efforts of programs in New York City.* NewYork: Institute for Urban and Minority Education.

Florida Department of Education (1996). *Dropout prevention: Annual report of program effectiveness, 1994-95 school year.* Tallahassee, FL: Florida Department of Education, Division of Public Schools.

Florida Kids Count Data Book (1994). *Florida center for children and youth.* Volume V.

Floyd, M. (1993). Teachers College, Columbia University, unpublished draft. *Mentoring. Education Research Consumer Guide,* No. 7.

Foley, E. (1983). Alternative schools: New findings. *Social Policy,* 13(3), 4-46.

Frymier, J. (1989). *A study of students at risk: Collaborating to do research.* Bloomington, IN: Phi Delta Kappa Educational Foundation.

Frymier, J., & Gansneder, B. (1989). The Phi Delta Kappa study of students at risk. *Phi Delta Kappan,* 71, 142-146.

Goldstein, A.P. (1991). *Delinquent gangs: A psychological perspective.* Champaign, IL: Research Press.

Goldstein, A.P., & Huff, C.R. (1993). *The gang intervention handbook.* Champaign, IL: Research Press.

Hamilton, S., & Hamilton M. (1992). Mentoring programs: Promise and paradox. *Phi Delta Kappan,* 546-550.

Harris, L. (1990). *A study of mentors and students in the career beginnings: Mentoring program.* New York: Common Wealth Fund.

Hefner-Packer, R. (1991). *Alternative education programs: A prescription for success. Monographs in Education.* Vol. 12, C.T. Holmes (Ed.). Athens, GA: College of Education, University of Georgia.

Hodgkinson, H. (1991). *Beyond the schools: How schools and communities must collaborate to solve the problems facing America's youth.* Indianapolis, IN: National Educational Service.

Holmes, T. C., & Matthews, K. M. (1984). Implications of regional cost adjustments to school finance plans. *Educational Administration Quarterly, 20*(1), 69-92.

Johnson, D., & Johnson, F.P. (1986). *Learning together and alone.* (2d ed.). Englewood Cliffs, NJ: Prentice Hall.

Kwalick, B. (1988). *Student mentor program: A collaborative program.* Mentor Handbook. Clemson, SC: National Dropout Prevention Center.

Laughrey, M. (1990). *The design and implementation of a mentor program to improve the academic achievement of black male high school students.* ERIC Reproduction Services, ED No. 328647.

Lefkowitz, B. (1989). *Tough charge: Growing up on your own in America.* New York: Free Press.

Lehr, J.B., & Harris, H. W. (1994). *At-risk, low achieving students in the classroom.* Washington, DC: National Education Association.

Manning, T. E. (1993). Life in the Nineties. *NCA Quarterly, 68*(2), 319-22.

Miller, J.W. (1993). *Students at risk: Pitfalls and promising plans.* Dubuque, IA: Brown Communications.

Mizxokawa, D.T. (1988). *Attributions of academic success and failure to effort or ability: A comparison of six Asian-American ethnic groups.* Paper presented at the American Educational Research Association.

Mordkwotiz E.R., & Ginsburg, H.P. (1986). *Early academic socialization of successful Asian-American college students.* Paper presented at the Annual Meeting of the American Educational Research Association.

Morley, R.E. (1993). *Alternative education: National Dropout Prevention Center dropout prevention research reports.* Clemson, SC: National Dropout Prevention Center.

National Assessment of Educational Progress (1985). *The reading report card: Progress toward excellence in our schools: Trends in reading over four national assessments 1971-1984.* Princeton, NJ: National Assessment of Educational Progress.

National Center for Educational Statistics (1990). *Dropout rates in the United States.* Washington, DC: U.S. Department of Education.

Ogden, E.H., & Ferminario, V. (1988). *The at-risk student: Answers for educators.* Lancaster, PA: Technomic Publishing Company, Inc.

Orr, T.M. (1987). *Keeping students in school.* San Francisco, CA: Jossey-Bass.

Pellicano, R. R. (1987). At risk: A view of social advantage. *Educational Leadership,* 44(6), 47-49.

Peng, S. S. (1983). *High school drop outs: Descriptive information from high school and beyond.* National Center for Educational Statistics Bulletin.

Raywid, M.A. (1994). Alternative schools: The state of the art. *Educational Leadership, 52*(2), 26-31.

Reglin, G.L. (1995). *Achievement for African-American Students: Strategies for the Diverse Classroom.* Indianapolis, IN: National Educational Service.

Reglin, G.L. (1993a). *Motivating low-achieving students: A special focus on unmotivated and underachieving African American students.* Springfield, IL: Charles C. Thomas.

Reglin, G.L. (1993b). *At-risk "parent and family" school involvement: Strategies for low income families and African-American families of unmotivated and underachieving students.* Springfield, IL: Charles C. Thomas.

Reglin, G.L. (1990). A model program for educating at-risk students. *T.H.E. Journal: Technological Horizons in Education, 17*(6), 65-67.

Richardson, V., Casanova, U., Placier, P., & Guilfoyle, K. (1989). *School children at-risk.* New York: The Falmer Press.

Richman, B.S. (1991). *School climate and restructuring for low-achieving students.* Philadelphia, PA: Research for Better Schools.

Rotter, J.B. (1975). Some problems and misconceptions related to the construct of internal versus external control of reinforcement. *Journal of Consulting and Clinical Psychology, 48,* 56-57.

Slavin, R.E. (1989). *Effective programs for students at risk.* Needham Heights, MA: Allyn and Bacon.

Stopp, H. (1996). M.A.T.H. project helps fight truancy. *Research (3),* 1.

Wircenski, J.L., Sarkees, M.D., & West, L.L. (1990). *Instructional alternatives: Rescue strategies for at-risk students.* Reston, VA: National Association of Secondary School Principals.

Young, T. (1990). *Public alternative education.* New York: Teachers College Press.